When Conscience Speaks

by
Christopher Riley

PublishAmerica
Baltimore

ISBN: 1-60441-685-8
PUBLISHED BY PUBLISHAMERICA, LLLP
www.publishamerica.com
Baltimore

Printed in the United States of America

To Anna, Junior, Ophelia, Octavia, and Samuel

To: Clova

from

Christoph Riley

13th August 2008

ACKNOWLEDGEMENT

I am very grateful to the following persons who have helped me while I was preparing this manuscript. They have each contributed in accordance to their background. However, the errors in this manuscript are mine alone.

Milan Kesel, a self confessed atheist, has read and encouraged me to complete this work. Though he questioned the strong Biblical content, he was always enthusiastic about the arguments. I thank Denna Carr, a Roman Catholic, who studied Theology, for her useful comments. I also thank my friend Shirley Roberts, a freelance journalist, for her suggestions on style.

Joe Gomez (my dear friend and *frater*) has been very supportive. I also thank Jennifer Rogers for her comments. As always, the several pastors, within the 'flocks' I served, have always encouraged me to complete this task. For it is their duty as shepherds to nurture the gifts and talents of all their church members.

I thank the Lord for my life and health for He alone has allowed me to spend many nights at the computer. Without energy and health, I would not have been able to do all the writing and re-writing of this manuscript that I have done. Still I am sure there must be areas that I can improve on or condense much more. There are other ideas that I could have included, but the book would be too big and would defeat the present purpose.

I am also grateful to Gisele McMillan, Dennis Morison, Ted Wallace, Andrew Scharfe, and Bill Ries. They all understand the mysteries of the computer.

TRUST YOUR SPIRIT

Heed the urges of your innerself.
Its voice is the conscience of God,
All truths, all laws, it thus enhance
For it communes with the Great Light, the Lord

Its riches are beyond the material
Its wisdom and understanding from above
Flamed to a success ethereal
then ashed in beauty, peace and love

We who ignore what God dictates
Is it not we, who are the victims of fate?
For denial to conform to an illumined suggestion
can result in the fulfilment of eternal damnation

Then what O man? You cry out…
with your trampled heart bursting in a shout
beseeching, "O Lord! Help me!"
Then you are rescued by His Mercy's decree

O doubtful man! Why are you so stubborn?
Why do you cause heartaches in abundance?
Is it not wiser to listen to your inner self,
instead of the tempter or someone else

TABLE OF CONTENTS

Introduction

Though to err is human, we cannot escape the pains and unpleasantness that we must experience as we compensate for our mistakes. For a system of recognizing and signalling of our errors is inborn and is con-created with our humanity. Therefore, our accountability is guaranteed, our punishment assured. Thus the torment of our conscience. We can neither hide behind this human quality of imperfection and wilfully commit acts against society and God. The flaw of our humanness does not excuse our errors, nor lessen our punishment. The law is exact and automatic. It does not discriminate. Further, along with our imperfections come our good natures. For our good thoughts and deeds, our rewards too are automatic. We feel the approval of conscience—it is *'gracefully clear.'*

But can we take personal credit for this so-called goodness of ours? By that I mean, can we boast that this goodness is natural in us or arises by our human effort? Were we born with a self-knowledge of right and wrong? Or did we accumulate what we know over time and with experiences? If so, why do we do wrong things so often? What is our apparent attraction to evil and sin anyway? Alternatively, what are the benefits—if any—when we do right? Why do we inwardly demand that we be rewarded for our good deeds? What is this right and wrong or good and bad we are so often concerned about?

We frequently act by choice or accident in accordance with God's laws and thus we are compensated with happiness, inner peace, and with material blessings or gifts. When we choose wrongly, we feel pain, disappointment, and sometimes unbearable torment from our conscience. Our heart aches. Thus along with the blessings are the curses—it would seem we cannot get one without the other. This is one of the major themes throughout the Holy Bible—even from as early as Genesis. For instance, we have also read why Noah had to build an Ark. Noah and his family served God and they were blessed—their lives were spared—while others died in a flood as they did not obey or serve the Lord of the Universe. One can only imagine the heart-wrenching, grappling, and desperate regret many must have felt while they were drowning, which was only too late—realizing that Noah was right to obey God. He was not a fool, after all, to build the Ark on dry land.

Disobedience—even from the beginning of time has been a dilemma. It still is today. But God still loves us. The Bible says that we all fall short of the glory of God (Romans 3:23). This is not a mere pessimistic view of humans, but the reality of our birthright of our relationship with God. None of us can dodge the clutches of imperfection. We are, in a sense, the equivalent to an unripened fruit. We are incomplete in our growth and in our inner make up. We observe even other philosophies and religions agree with this truism. So just like the sweet or sour taste of a fruit results from its inner constituents, so our character depends upon the content of our being. That is, as the life sap gives the fruit its taste, so our inner values form and shape our character. Hence if these values are soiled or tarnished, so would our character and human nature be, just as the poor manure would grow undernourished fruits. It follows then that we would possess a questionable conscience because of our sinful, immoral nature.

It is not surprising that most of us have heard the following statements before. "If I could live my life over," and "I wish I had the opportunities in life which my children now have." These are statements of regret and wishful thinking. They have two implications. The first, is that God is unfair to provide the youths today with opportunities that people did not have yesterday. The second, is that we think what we have accomplished in our lives to date is inadequate. But there is an underlying assumption that if we are allowed to live our lives over, we would do things differently. There is an old adage, in a Tibetan book scroll called *Unto Thee I Grant*, that rhetorically questions, why should humans ask the Creator for an extended or another life. For would we not sin more, suggests the Tibetan ancients? Undoubtedly our natures are still imperfect and so our judgement will continue to be fallible. We must agree with the "old adage" above.

I have also heard a few people say they will die in peace because they believe they have really lived full lives. Have they? How do they know? By what measurements have they determined that they have fulfilled their life's missions? What if they short changed themselves and they did not know? For their value-judgements could have been faulty and so the inner approvals they received from their consciences would have been wrong. Nonetheless, the point here is that their accomplishments in life make them, upon reflection, smile and feel proud. They may not have left their footprints in the history books and be known as famous men or women, nevertheless, whatever they have done, they believe it to be important enough. Thus they are happy with how they have lived. In the end, they go to their graves in peace—though it may be illusory or temporary. Only God knows.

Could it be then that God was good to some and not to others? Shall we then accuse our Lord of being bias? If we fail our examinations because we did not know how to solve some problems, who is to blame? If we choose an apple off a vendor's stand, pay for it and find it rotten inside, who is to blame? God? No. It is our own bad choices and decisions. This book does not deal with such actual experiences of say an innocent child being raped or born incapacitated; nor does it attempt to address the conundrum of if God is alive when some God-fearing innocent young person is being murdered. An examination of those realities are perhaps better addressed under the doctrine of predestination, free will, and glorifying God. I leave that for the writers on issues dealing with universal principles of justice, love, God's free will, and His acts of mercy.

In this book I am dealing with the living. That is, the art of living life in a manner that pleases and honours God. In other words, making choices and decisions in harmony with the dictates of a theonomous or Christlike conscience. David said in his Psalms that we cannot praise God in our graves (Ps. 6:5). Solomon said that while we are alive, we must enjoy our lives, our families, and do our duties to God (Eccl. 9:9; 12:13b). These are the ways in which we can honour God in our obedience and recognition of His sovereignty.

Notice that when we win or achieve any measure of success, we say, "I have done it." We may also boast, "I have won over the others." We may even, with apparent modesty, state, "I did the best I possibly could under the circumstances." We often do not give any credit to God—the Almighty Provider, the Divine Principle, through whom we accomplish everything. Let us remember the parable of the ten lepers healed by Jesus. Only one returned to thank him. And Jesus deliberately and pedagogically wondered why **only** '*the foreigner*' returned "to give praise to God" (Luke 17:11-19). Supposedly the other nine hopped and skipped away with joy about their healing and forgot to show gratitude to Jesus for healing them. This is indeed disappointing and regrettable. But is not such ingratitude the norm today as it has been since the beginning—biblically speaking? Of course there is a larger message here, which we are not presently concerned with. We are now focussed on gratitude. Does it not bother us to be thankful? In the parable, should not the leper feel guilt and regret for not showing their gratitude?

We easily forget the goodness and favours we receive. We are quick, and without hesitation, to accept responsibility and praise for our good or successful deeds. We speak of creative talents and urges, forgetting Solomon, the wise, saying that there is nothing new under the sun. We should remember or become aware of philosophy's discussion on synthesis and psychology's on synthetic creation. Some literally and *creaturely* argue that to create is *doubtful* and *unprovable*. It means producing "something" from "nothing." This is only possible, they contend, if we confer a reality on the so-called "nothing" or "no thing." But why is it so difficult to believe that God, who created the world and us, can also act outside human logic and reason? This is one of the pet peeves of secular philosophy, but a foundational pillar of theology: '*that a supreme and infinite God, who necessarily must exist, has created the world and all existences or beings.*'

Thus we need God in the equation of life. We need His Universal Intelligence, His transcendent and immanent Consciousness for anything to happen in our lives. How many of us say "Thank God, I was successful" and really know that it is because of Him we succeed? "Thank God" has become a passing conventional expression like "Good morning." That is, it has become an involuntary rather than a voluntary acknowledgement of our gratitude to our Lord and Master. Once our hearts have become so complacent—having no affections—we then react as if we possess no conscience.

Each day, each moment in our lives, we face decisions. These determine what our position will be tomorrow or next year. What we do today, will mean a smile or a cry in the days ahead. What we accept or reject could be our ticket to a better life, our entry into hard times, or our receiving eternal life or contempt. During these swift and decisive moments, our consciences are duty bound. It causes us to know if our thoughts and deeds, choices and decisions, are right or wrong by "*filling*" us with remorse, guilt, regret, or approval. These decisions, these choices—along with your responses to the Holy Spirit—are important to us because they are our only hope for the salvation of our soul personality, which Jesus Christ has appropriated and given freely.

For the purposes of the discussion in this book, it matters not if we refer to ourselves as a body, soul, spiritual self, soul personality, or maintain the Hebraic and biblical understanding of a human being. The terminology will not in any way affect the reality that we all have a conscience and we are all accountable for how we 'treat' this divinely endowed principle. Treatment here refers to how we train conscience; what values do we give it; and how we respond to its promptings and judgements.

When we cry because we lost our lover, it may be because we

made the wrong choice sometime in our past. Perhaps too, we may have either spoken or acted wrongfully, or we may have made the grave mistake of choosing the wrong partner—in the first place. In looking back: did we nurture conscience with what we read, studied, experienced, and believed? Did we listen to its voice? Did we get its approval or guilt in our considerations?

By our decisions we '*create*' relationships. They grow and die because of our right or wrong choosing. If we lack the proper information at the start, if we are impatient and careless, we will make many mistakes which will cause us much heartaches. A discerning spirit helps us to determine which voice within is speaking and to which we must listen. Is it conscience, the Holy Spirit, Satan, our reasoning mind and logic, the memory of what a friend or author said and concluded on a situation?

In the following discussion, we will deal with those aspects of relationships with ourselves, God, and nature. In these, our conscience plays a vital role. If we listen with careful consideration to our **righteous** conscience—our personal inner guardian, we find profound peace and happiness. But if we disobey when our conscience prompts us, by changing our decisions or actions, we would later regret. We would then live with disgrace and shame.

Since the beginning with Adam, disobedience brings sadness, regret, and *spiritual death*. Our relation with God is thwarted by *the evil one*. If the law is written in our hearts or conscience and we violate it, we too will lose all our joys and promised benefits (Genesis 3:17, 19, 23). But the Holy Bible offers us hope as descendents of Abraham along with a plan of action when we **choose to imitate Christ**. Our conscience, when imbued with the contents of the Heart and Mind of God, will truly direct us to the good life.

Conscience is viewed and discussed herein, from an orthodox evangelical context. At once we realise the suggested differences due to the many flavours of Christianity. There are many sects and denominations, each with variations of the doctrines and sometimes interpretations of the Holy Scriptures. Even that too is worth our careful choosing as we have many biblical versions. Each of us must determine with wisdom whether the Bible we choose is authentic.

It is from this point our difficulty starts. How to know which biblical version is authentic? In this book, I have accepted the view that most versions are authentic and we can arrive at the best meanings of a text or verse of Scripture by comparing how the text is expressed in different Bibles. The main version referenced here is the New International Version (NIV). There are several good books and courses one can take on how to read and interpret the Bible correctly as well as how to choose a proper study Bible. It is my view that they all essentially present the core gospel message and the *Lordship, authority,* and *saving work* of Christ Jesus. We have some extreme exceptions, of course, but it is not the place in this current text to deal with the topic of "distorted biblical interpretations."

My target audience comprises the orthodox evangelical community. As a Christian and Christian Educator I believe that an understanding of conscience within an evangelical Christian context is important in our walk with Christ. Conscience is related to morals. It is these value standards that give it impetus and provide us with the tools to recognize the guiding principles upon which it is based. We are bounded by the behaviour of Jesus Christ as articulated and directly implied in the Holy Bible.

We recognise this Bible as God's *complete* and *infallible* Word. We acknowledge that the Scriptures were inspired by God and written by men chosen by Him and who wrote under the direct supervision of His Holy Spirit. The challenge of this book, *When Conscience Speaks*, is to help us to *engage* our conscience to be sensitive and to be in accord with the Holy Scriptures and in the pleasure of Jesus Christ. It is for this reason my focus has been the use of biblical references rather than on the *myriad* philosophical, other religious, and psychological views on conscience.

Conscience—A Gift from God

Except for children's cartoons, I cannot think of any instance when an animal was tormented by its conscience. I have neither read nor been exposed to any data whereby predator animals were tormented by their conscience after hunting and then devouring their preys. The Bible does not have a single instance that indicates the presence of conscience in animals—unless of course, I have missed it. The faculty of conscience appears to be one of the distinctiveness of human beings. In all walks of life, people speak of and refer to conscience as a central principle of integrity. It is as if conscience is universally accepted as an incorruptible part of human nature—people swear by it, give evidence by it, and make assurances in politics and in relationships by it.

That said, many confer upon it a divine quality. On the other hand, those who offer us a psychological explanation to our good and bad behaviour, see conscience only as a mere creation of our evolving human personality or ego. They claim that conscience is a necessary formulation for human and societal order and survival. There is one final group of persons who is adamant in its opposing view that humans can survive or exist without a conscience as evident in the behaviour of a hardened criminal personality.

Taking this last group first, these persons do not stress the role of conscience. In fact, they feel that a person can live without one as can be seen in the lives of murderous individuals or even in con-artists who deliberately and repeatedly rip-off innocent victims. Such people, who wantonly commit perfidious and evil acts, replaced conscience with a matrix of whims and matching relevant satisfaction. So-called conscienceless people would include too, those politicians who use their authority and military power to enslave and oppress their citizens. We can add, the employers who knowingly underpay their employees—leaving the latter in such poverty wherein they cannot even pay for their needed medication or buy enough food to *barely* escape the grip of starvation.

Obviously, if we perceive anyone as having "no conscience," we infer an understanding that conscience resides only in the human beings who are 'good.' Such persons have morals and thus recognize the value of right and wrong, but who would naturally choose to do 'the right thing.' Meanwhile the immoral person normally chooses 'the wrong thing—*at least wrong by commonly accepted social values and standards.*' These immoral individuals do have some sense of right and wrong. To them, sin is sweet. They acquired a *taste* for it—it became their natural choice.

I am not a psychologist, but a Christian Educator. From a Biblical perspective, these immoral persons behave like reprobate souls. "[God] gave them over," according to Apostle Paul, "…to a depraved mind…" (Rom. 1:28; see 1:25, 29-32). But we must notice too, that these persons "although they know God's righteous decree…, they not only continue [in their so-called conscienceless activities],…but also approve of those who practice them" (Rom. 1:32). Therefore, these persons, know what is right, but simply and wickedly choose to do wrong. They do have a conscience. Yet, superficially speaking, with this view we imply that, some persons do and others do not. The connotation is that not all persons are born with a conscience—if it at all exists from birth.

Next we come to those who perceive this conscience as a necessary learned set of standards called morals. This is the view that dominated psychology for many years and which universities teach in Psychology 101 (Introduction to Psychology). There have since been some changes. However, it was first explained by the infamous Psychologist, Sigmund Freud. To him, conscience and morality are a natural link. He taught that the internalisation of parental prohibitions and demands leads to the development of a conscience or *superego*.

In this view, the notion of the universal moral law is *excluded*. So what individuals are taught as right and wrong by their parents and those in authority become these persons' standards and morals. Be that as it may, this view does in fact accept that the person eventually has some form of inner automatic response system that evaluates and judges the persons' thoughts and actions. Thus the Freudian conscience is heteronomous—arising from external controls and impositions initially outside itself. This view, like the previous one, does not address the importance of whether an individual was born with a conscience. From our over simplified explanation of superego, no individual is born with a conscience. Rather, conscience is developed from a child to maturity.

A third view of conscience is pantheistic in perception. This means that conscience is part of 'God that is within us.' In other words, it is part of the divine spark within humans. Put another way, conscience is the inner guardian, the master within. These terminologies can sometimes become confusing and misleading so let us first state that "pantheism," as defined by the Merriam-Webster's Collegiate Dictionary—11th edition, "equates God with the forces and the laws of the universe." Still, there may be slight variations to the interpretation of the meaning of pantheism. For instance, another flavour of pantheism may also espouse that the divine essence permeates all existences. Yet these pantheists may perceive God or Divine Mind as different from the cosmic, universal laws.

Thus with this latter varied definition, conscience is not God but god, but the master within for that individual. This variation does not change the fact of the autonomy of conscience, but it emphasises the 'guardian role' of conscience in that person. In this third view, individuals are born with a conscience and it is the final and personal authority of right and wrong for that individual. Conscience here is thus **autonomous**. The New Age, some esoteric schools, and some eastern religions would be in sync with this view.

Both autonomous and heteronomous conscience can accommodate laws approving homosexuality, lesbianism, same-sex marriage, transsexual orientation, euthanasia, abortion, situation ethics (as necessary lie, justified killings), ethnic cleansing, slavery, apartheid policies, and suicide bombings. In the autonomous conscience, if humankind is god, then one can do as one pleases within the context of one's understanding and interpretation of cosmic laws. With heteronomous conscience, once there is a societal consensus in which no one is hurt, then one can have approval for any value that meets this requirement. Freedom to exercise one's religious beliefs has legally and officially allowed witchcraft, Satanism, and other unnatural religious systems. The heteronomous conscience will allow the legalising of prostitution as it may provide, for instance, additional taxes, monitored and controlled venereal diseases in sex shops, and a livelihood for some people.

The last view of conscience we will consider, the orthodox evangelical view, is Biblical. It is the view held throughout this book. It holds that conscience is a gift from God to humanity. This is a theonomous view in the sense that conscience can work in harmony with God's laws, provided the individual is under the direction of the Holy Spirit. Conscience is not God; but can be subjected to God's Will when one is a believer in the Lordship of Jesus Christ. As the Apostle Paul says, "I speak the truth in Christ—I am not lying, my conscience confirms it in the Holy Spirit..."(Rom. 9:1). Thus he speaks with a theonomous conscience.

It is only in the New Testament that the use of the word 'conscience' appears; but it is alluded to repeatedly in the Old Testament often when the word 'heart' or 'spirit' is used. Take the example of Remises, the infamous hard hearted Egyptian Pharaoh, who refused to free God's people, no matter the repeated pleas of Moses (Ex. 7-12). Pharaoh's pride, stubbornness, and determination to challenge the will of God have blinded his reason and have made his regal rulings folly. His confidence and convictions that he was right were imprisoned by the walls of his heartlessness or seared conscience. We can look too at the Scripture which stated that God removed the Holy Spirit from Saul who disobeyed God repeatedly (1 Sam. 16:14-15). The Bible tells us that God sent an evil spirit to torment Saul (v. 14b). Clearly Saul's torment was heartfelt. In today's language, we will say that 'his conscience bothered or troubled him.'

At times too, by the very behaviour of people we can posit the workings of conscience. When God was calling Adam and Eve in the Garden of Eden, they hid from Him (Gen. 3:8-10). The reason they gave, was due to their nakedness. Was that then the nakedness of their physical bodies? Or can we also proffer, hermeneutically speaking of course, that 'nakedness' can mean the obviousness of their wrong, or the guilt they felt upon *His Presence*? After all, God is **The Truth** (Jn. 14:6) and He is **Holy** (Lev. 11:44; 1 Pe. 1:15, 16).

They knew they sinned against Him; they were ashamed. But I suggest the larger issue is not there *physical* nakedness, but *their disobedience* in juxtaposition of their knowledge of truth that caused them to realise they were naked. God said, "What is this you have done (Gen. 3:13)?" Of course the Bible tells us they were naked, for they covered themselves with "sewed fig leaves" (Gen. 3:7). If this is *simply* exegetically literal in meaning, why should they be ashamed and "afraid" (Gen. 3:10) to stand physically naked before the one who created them—who is omnipresent? They knew they did something wrong: not being naked, but sinned against God. God then gave them better and more permanent clothing (vv. 21), and thereafter drove them out of the Garden of Eden (vv. 23).

Conscience is implicit from the very beginning, and it is an integral part of repentance which is a necessary reality in the Salvation plan (Lev. 5:5). For instance, it is the tormenting of our conscience that wounds us with a resounding and excruciating pain, signalling us with the following guilt, regret, or remorse. The penitence we experience arises out of the workings of our conscience. The Holy Spirit convicts us and conscience signals, thus causing our resultant repentance. This leads to our humbly seeking forgiveness from God through our lord Jesus Christ.

An additional question one may pose is: do children have conscience? That is, are humans born with conscience or is it a faculty that is conferred upon us as we become more akin to the material and sinful world? Of course, from the very definition by psychology of conscience or superego, the answer is "no." *Merriam-Webster's Collegiate Dictionary* defines the word amoral as "being neither moral or immoral or as lying outside the sphere to which moral judgements apply." As an example, the dictionary states, "infants are amoral." The infant has made no moral judgement. However, this does not mean that the child is sinless.

The Holy Bible, God's inerrant and infallible Word (Prov. 30:5), tells us that we were born in sin. The psalmist David said, "Surely I was sinful at birth, sinful from the time my mother conceived me." (Ps. 51:5). And Paul said "...for all have sinned and fall short of the glory of God" (Rom. 3:23). At what point during childhood did the infant do wrong, the sceptic may ask? This question is not unique, for the disciples themselves asked Jesus that very question when they came upon a man who was blind from birth (Jn. 9:1-3). They assumed the man or his parents sinned because their Jewish Theologians taught that the retributive cause of *sickness* was *sin*—either **parental** or **prenatal** sin. Jesus changed and then answered the question, **not what**, but **why** 'was the man blind from birth.' The answer Christ gave was "to glorify God" (Jn. 9:3). The Bible, which is Truth, tells us Adam brought sin into the world (Rom. 5:12-14). How much clearer must the Word of God be? The Apostle Paul says, "There is no one righteous, not even one...there is no one who does good, not even one..." (Rom. 3:10, 12b). Thus the propensity to sin is in all humans from birth—its part of our Old Nature which we inherited from Adam (Rom. 5:12).

We might ask, 'What is the relationship between our sinful nature and conscience—if there is one at all?' Sin in humans is not a natural part of how God wants us to be. He created human beings without sin—in His own image (Gen. 1: 27). We have seen that sin was brought into the world by Adam. When we comply with a sinful prompting, we become accountable to God for our wrong choosing. In the face of the Moral Law, we transgress and our inside or something inside of us hurts and we know "we messed up." Our

23

right or wrong thoughts and actions appear to turn on a switch to a subsequent inner process that produces a relevant 'good or bad' feeling inside us. That *process or something* inside us is our conscience. How did it come into being?

We know God in His grace and mercy, established a salvation plan for us to return to good fellowship with Him (Gen. 3:15). We recognize His perfect intelligence, character, and plans. Even in His judgement, He is fair and complete. Thus He foreknew our weaknesses, strengths, and needs. With Adam's condemnation (Gen. 3:17) and humanity's curse (Rom. 5:12), God knew our sinful nature *and* a Moral Law *cannot* be mutually exclusive. Without the law we would not know if we sinned. Paul was clear when he said, "Indeed I would not have known what sin was except through the law (Rom. 7:7)."

Naturally, 'the knowledge or recognition of sin' (of which Paul speaks), infers the use of intellect, mind, memory, and sensitivity (or consciousness). In Romans 7, Paul talks about the interplay of good and evil with our human nature and with reference to the law (vv. 21). He also inferred significant value of our related emotional responses when he, for instance, says, "…in my inner being I delight in God's law…(vv.22)." He continued saying, "What a wretched man I am! Who will rescue me…(vv. 24)." Evidently, the interplay of sin and law produces 'defining emotional responses—much like conscience.' Thus, we not only have knowledge of our wrong doing, we 'feel' the wrongfulness or rightfulness of our thoughts and actions. Hence it is logical to assume that God, in His Perfect Wisdom, did create human beings with conscience from birth.

Whether a solid faculty that is substantive or a matrix imbued with consciousness and the ability to determine right from wrong, we have showed that conscience does have a definite relationship with sin. Added to this, we saw that conscience relates to sin in collaboration with the Moral Law. Put in the negative, conscience is useless if sin or the Moral Law existed by themselves; but has logical significance when both are in juxtaposition. So far science has not dissected any physical organ and identified it as conscience. I am unaware of any textbook on physiology that has declared a specific part of the human anatomy as the conscience. Conscience exists, so we all claim with conviction, yet we cannot discern it with our peripheral senses. But in every world religion, we acknowledge that conscience is real—even atheists and agnostics accept its existence. Philosophers and psychologists too. Perhaps that is what the Greek philosopher Socrates was referring to when he spoke of an inner divine spark that tells him if he is making a wrong decision.

The Apostle Paul says, in Romans 7, that sin is in us but is only because of the law that its existence is realised. Without the law, says Paul, we would have no cognisance that sin is in us. In fact, the psalmist says, "Oh how I love your law, I meditate on it all day long…" (Ps. 119:97) and in verse 11, he says, "I have hidden your word in my heart that I might not sin against you." Here is a confirmation that the presence of the law first makes us aware and able to distinguish that which is sinful; and two, this law convicts us and can help to prevent us from violating the will and wishes of God.

This law, to which Paul constantly refers, must be a universal law. Having to do with right and wrong, it must therefore be the law of the Lord (Ps. 119:1), His statutes (vv. 2), His precepts (vv. 4), and His decrees (vv. 8). This law is eternal. It is, to some extent, innate in all humans and allows us to know how to distinguish between good from evil and right from wrong. No matter the differences in our cultures, religious beliefs, birthplaces, genders, or education, we all seem to have many similar understanding of what is true, false, honest, dishonest, good or bad. This law, it seems, is written in the hearts of humans upon birth and we recognize it once we acquire some level of understanding (Rom. 2:14-15; Rom. 1:20; 1 Cor. 8:6).

The idea of God is also known to all humans (Rom. 1). Thus people claiming to be atheists deceive themselves. The Bible unequivocally calls them 'fools.' Scripture says, "The fool says in his heart, there is no God" (Ps. 14:1). Further, Scripture says many persons in their pride are wicked and do not seek God, and "…in all [their] thoughts there is no room for God" (Ps. 10:4). When we know God, we know His laws in our hearts and in our being. Long before puberty we have a general idea of what is right and wrong. Long before he was born, God knew how contentious Ishmael, the first son of Abraham, would be (Gen. 16:12). In Rebekah's womb, Isaac and Esau "jostled each other." God said, it is because "…the older would serve the younger" (Gen. 25: 22-23).

God knows our tendencies before we are born. The greater our maturity, the greater our acquaintance with God's moral law operative within us. Surely, one may argue that much is learned from our parents, elders, and society in which we are born (and that is true); but no one can deny that quite often we even notice in children under the age of five years old that some are less or more selfish than others and that some are more obedient than others too. The average parent and adult can validate this common experience. That the law is operative within every child is an indisputable fact.

This law affects us and we first react in a somewhat emotional manner. When we do right we feel good inside and when we do wrong we feel bad. This good or bad feeling in us has a psychosomatic effect and it is what we generally call the expressions of our conscience. We, for instance, may at times feel pain in our hearts when our conscience torments us.

The child at birth or even at one year old is not self conscious. There are parts of their physical bodies of which they are unaware. Children would generally be responsive and sensitive to any external probing of their bodies as well as they would react to such stimuli as hunger from inside their bodies. Psychology states that children are in need of love and may even have mental, emotional problems without this love they need. That they have heart or lungs or kidneys inside of them is not known to them. That they have a circulation and respiratory system is also unknown to them. So too the faculty of conscience is unknown to them early in life. Perhaps conscience is a subject at this point which may best be addressed by the child psychologist; but as humans we daily deal with conscience and we often speak of it as it affects us in the humdrum affairs of our lives.

Conscience, we conclude, must have been con-created with our bodies. We know it exists as it is the outcome of the interaction of sin in us, the law that is written in our hearts, along with the application of our free will. Indeed it is a gift of God. It can guide us and keep us on the straight path. It is a product of His grace and mercy. He has given us all we need to return to that great covenant relationship we are meant to have with Him. We have salvation through Christ; free will to love and obey God; and conscience well trained to keep us balancing as we walk the tightrope of life back into the arms and to the side of our God.

It is true we may at times judge the evil, wretched, and vile acts of a past dictator as from a person with 'no conscience.' The implication here is that conscience by its very existence in us always exists for a good. It is there to help us to stay on the path to God through salvation by Christ Jesus. It is a blessing from God and all that He represents. Therefore, the evil minded, we conclude must be devoid of conscience. But this is untrue. For by our free will, we can learn to love evil and habitually perform acts against the good and holy purposes of God. And by repetition of a vile conduct, we make such evil behaviour the new law of our being. When we make evil our constant companion—we imbue it into our consciousness. Our conscience knows it as the truth (though it is twisted and false in reality) and so the pain we cause others do not bother us; their sorrows do not cause compassion to rise within us; and in their misfortunes, we feel neither pity nor sympathy nor even empathy for them. It is as if our feelings are dead.

For whatever the reason, which we shall later discuss, we at times are "broken" and weak; our will is in the arms of God's power; we are submissive to His Will, and we for a moment have a glimpse of His Love. Then a feeling of penitence and sorrow and lastly regret may overcome us. Here at last our conscience of the good in us arises victoriously. We were once evil and now we are good, by God's love emanating through us. Our strong will is broken and we yield to God's goodness and values. Our remorse indicates that we recognise the truth: it is not that we did not have a conscience; rather, it is that the good in us was hidden as sin thrived. We then, putting our burden in Christ Jesus and then letting him take the weight of our sins, evil, and troubles, are free and so the law no longer binds us.

Biblically, the human being is a personal unity. We are not comprised of body, mind, consciousness, will, soul, conscience and more. Orthodox Christian Theologians state that exegetically, the Bible presents a Hebraic understanding of human nature. That is, human beings are animated bodies, as God breathed the breath of life into their physical bodies. Therefore terminologies as soul, spirit, and flesh refer, not to parts of the human being; but are representative of the types of relationships we have with God. It is Greek philosophy that put into Christian theology the notion that the nature of humanity comprises a soul, body, spirit and so on. Hence we have the dichotomous and trichotomous views of humanness. This clarification is important to us as we must not view conscience as part of this composite, but as inclusive in the orthodox view of our human nature as a ***personal unity***. In other words, the Christian view is not that the body is physical and the soul is immaterial along with the spirit which is eternal and ever a part of God; but it is that the human being is *one animated whole*.

We observe in Genesis that Eve first recognised that what Satan initially suggested was a direct violation of God's command. She says, "…but God did say, 'You must not eat fruit from the tree that is in the middle of the garden, and you must not touch it, or you will die'" (Gen. 3:3). But Satan convinced her that God lied to her (v. 4). The truth is, says Satan persuasively, by eating of the 'forbidden fruit,' Eve's "…eyes will be opened and [she] will be like God, knowing good and evil" (v. 5b). She conceded and later convinced Adam to disobey (Gen. 3:6).

The questions is, did Adam and Eve ***knowingly*** and ***deliberately*** disobey God, or were they *at that point in time* thinking they were only complying with a variation of God's command or simply conceding to follow an alternative path? We must remember that they did not *at that time* know the difference between good and evil (as implied in Gen. 3:5); but they were aware that they were not doing what God told them to (see Gen. 3: 1-3). That Adam and Eve were naked is fact. They were only aware of this after eating the fruit (v. 7a).

Indeed, not only their physical bodies were naked, but their hearts, deeds, character, and personalities were naked. These were always crystal clear to the Eyes of God—that is, to the mind, intelligence, and consciousness of God. Adam and Eve heard God walking in the Garden of Eden means they suddenly become aware of The Symbol and sum total reality of The Moral Law (v. 8). This means that good and evil, right and wrong have dawned upon them. They were aware of their disobedience, they were aware of their sins.

Let us remember that Paul spoke of the law that has made him realise what sin is and that he was a sinner and there was always a tension in him between sin and goodness. Upon the realization of this tension, it is incumbent upon us to choose. This choice brings a natural emotional response from our conscience—one of which is guilt. The law of harmony and balance—of right and wrong—is here at work. When we obey, our entire being is in unison with God, His Laws, and all creation. An inward sense of approval and goodness we do feel. But when we disobey, we are out of tune with God, His Laws, and all creation. This imbalance is signalled by our conscience, which must have been created by God who knows our needs in the past, present and the future. For by His Grace and Mercy we are given free will to love and obey Him; and by that same Grace and Mercy, He gave us conscience to help clearly signal our rights and wrongs.

The Nature of Conscience

In this world where the highly evolved *soul personalities* or individuals dwell and have a personal and spiritual relationship with God, their responses to questions are either a confident "I know," or "I do not know." Their ignorance is not a sign of immaturity, nor a result of lack of thought or in-depth search for an answer to the respective question. Rather, it is an acknowledgement that there still exist so-called "secrets of God"—sometimes called "mysteries of life." Such "secrets" or "mysteries" are truths that are beyond our present human capacity to comprehend. Perhaps as we become more evolved, they will be "secrets" or "mysteries" no more; but join our font of universal principles and laws.

These "secrets" constitute knowledge of the universe for which either an individual human is "not ready," in terms of spiritual development to understand; or it is a body of knowledge that humanity is not yet evolved to accept. Therefore in facing decisions and making choices, how are we to know what is right from wrong? How are we to be certain that we are putting our feet in the right direction? Who or what will guide us? Who or what can show, whisper, caution, or speak to us in *golden silence* that we may know and be sure we are right—especially as some knowledge is beyond our reach? Is the answer conscience? If so, are we saying that conscience is a kind of god, and that it is all-knowing? Are we saying, everyone's conscience has *the right* answers?

What we do know is that conscience is alive within each of us. It is our personal shepherd. It is our radar and alarm system. It is a conscious and intelligible network of laws and principles like that of God's. Some appropriately calls it the master within and the inner guardian. It evaluates circumstances much more rapidly than does our objective reasoning. It answers in such silence that we have no choice but to recognize its humility and temperance. And yet we may criticise someone as having no conscience when they show no compassion; and others of having weak consciences when they yield to immoral conduct; and still some claim to have clear consciences, when they feel no remorse. It would seem we relate conscience with morals. The actions and reactions of our consciences are based on our individual moral values.

Conscience does not try to order us about nor does it even force nor sarcastically reprimand us. It prompts, guides, warns, and nags or torments. We may obey or disobey now. But in the next moment, conscience does not reproach us nor forget nor refuse to tell us, so that we feel and know right from wrong. Its behaviour is automatic and it is actuated because of consciousness—sensitivity and responsivity. We have given conscience a reality that functions in our objective and awakened state. Our consciences may well be functioning while we are asleep, but if it does, it has no effect on us such that we are aware—unless of course, it operates in our dream state. Such activity may not be of any conscious value to us, unless it plagues us behind the scenes when we are awake. What is certain is that our conscience never fails to respond to us—and perhaps, on our behalf. After all, it provokes an emotional overflow, causing a pleasant or unpleasant feeling which oftentimes leads to some external deed or utterance.

In 1981, we held a farewell party for a fellow security officer, who our company transferred to another school. During the party, he asked the principal, "Sir, how well would you say the security officers of our company have been performing?" The principal thought carefully and then said, "Given the training you have had, and considering the situations handled in this school, I think the officers have performed well."

I stood up and said that the principal did not say how well a job he thought our organization was doing. I felt that he did not directly answer the question. The principal replied to me with an analogy, using the movie, "The Day Of The Jackal." He said, "The investigators in the movie had many years of experience and training. They, therefore, handled the difficult situations competently." As he continued his analogy, his message became clear. He was saying that more competence and professionalism would depend upon the training and experience of the security officers of our company. However, I remained with the impression that he felt there was still much room for improvement.

I believe that our conscience performs similarly to the officers as in the example above. We must train our conscience. We must take the truths from our life experience and put them in our conscience knowledge-banks. Surely these truths are refined with the evolution of our personalities. I am suggesting that as we evolve we become closer to God or the Ultimate Reality. Thus our development causes our consciences to reflect judgements in harmony with God's Laws. The Bible tells us to receive God's word and lay it up in our hearts and souls (Deuteronomy 11:18). By doing this, we are ensuring that the internal auditor of our thoughts and actions becomes progressively more reliable. The habit of "putting" God's word in our hearts will naturally put his values in the centre of our mind and consciousness and so our consciences will be conversant of His Ways. Hence our consciences will operate relative to the level and degree of training we give it.

From experience and referring to the Holy Scriptures, we can say there are four general ways in which our conscience expresses itself. Each way reflects the state or nature of our individual conscience. Such expressions are the results of the interactions between situations inside and outside ourselves and our innermost values.

No individual displays only one of the expressions of conscience. In different circumstances we may show one or a combination of two or more ways of how conscience expresses itself. We may reveal a weak, strong, clear, or seared conscience—either as a pro-action or as a reaction.

In 1 Corinthians 8, the Apostle Paul tells us not to eat the meat that has been placed as a sacrifice to an idol. For if a brother of a "weaker conscience" sees us do it, he may think what he has seen us done is right. Then later, he may emulate us. Thus we have caused him to sin. Here Paul obviously implies that the value judgements within the brother of a weaker conscience will not be in harmony with God Laws. The weaker brother's conscience reflects the level of development of his personality and the training the brother gave his conscience. Clearly this brother's process of evaluation includes the reasoning that the elder must know what is right and thus all he needs to do is to follow suit rather than independently evaluate and decide for himself. This decision making of the conscience reminds us of the operations of a computer described by the acronym GIGO (Garbage In Garbage Out). This means that the computer cannot make accurate calculations and predictions if its input is faulty.

Returning to Paul's statement in 1 Corinthians 8, we note that nothing is wrong with the meat, except that the one watching may not clearly understand that the idol is only a physical, powerless object. The observer may also misunderstand that those using the meat to prepare the sacrifice are unaware that the idol is powerless. They may also be unaware that all sacrifices should glorify the one living, Universal God. The brother of weak conscience is himself without the proper knowledge and thus anyone can easily mislead him.

If we are daily watchful of our moral conducts and ethics, we can build a strong conscience filled with God's righteousness. As much as possible, we must live clean lives and hold pure thoughts. We must hide the Holy Scriptures in our hearts as the Psalmist says (Psalm 119:11). In this way, our conscience will easily be in harmony with the will of God. This is indeed a strong conscience: the kind that will allow us to shun evil as God commands in the Holy Scriptures(1 Thessalonians 5:22). The Scriptures would identify for us a working list of what is and is not evil. Nothing much is new that is happening under the sun. Many of the past sins still exist in some varied form today. Quohelet (who some claims to be Solomon the wisest man in the world) begins his book in Ecclesiastes 1:9-10 as there is nothing new under the sun. Hence being conversant with biblical precepts will undoubtedly keep us in check with right and wrong. Thus giving us a strong conscience—one illumined by God. Scripture says, in 2 Tim. 3:16 that the Bible should be used for "correction."

The Bible says, "Eat everything sold in the meat market without raising questions of conscience, for, 'The earth is the Lord's and everything in it'" (1 Corinthians 10:25,26). As we know that God created everything on earth and all belongs to Him; we cannot be wrong in eating "everything sold in the meat market." Although the things are sacrificed to some inanimate idol, we must realise that the idol cannot do anything by and of itself. We should ignore what anyone else may say or think in this regard. We may only refuse to eat the meat from the market, if and only if, our actions may cause another of weaker conscience to get the wrong impression.

Sometimes our actions are right, but others watching us still get the wrong impression. If we know this and continue with what we are doing, we show how insensitive we are. With this insensitivity, we give ourselves over to sensuality so as to indulge in every kind of impurity, with a continual lust for more (Ephesians 4:19). Further, we show how undoubtedly seared our conscience is. Here we show a blatant disregard to the principle of being our brother's keeper (John 15:12). This attitude is anti-Christ or a show of anti-biblical values. Such is from a personality whose morals are vile, base, and derelict.

Let us consider as an extreme example the criminal. He commits illegal acts without having any remorse. We may wonder how is it possible for him to sleep at nights. Our mere considering of his actions may keep us awake, while he may be having a full night's rest. His conscience does not operate at the level of an individual whose heart is set on God. His conscience and mind are corrupt and seared (Titus 1:15). Naturally, his conduct and morals will differ from those who stand by the values of what is right and wrong in the Christian Bible.

If we are highly moral persons or we are ardent bible believing, faith seeking understanding persons, on the other hand, we could not sleep if we have hurt someone or done something wrong—morally or legally. We would have trained our minds and hearts to know the truths and results of right and wrong behaviour. Once we have done what is right, we feel at ease. For we have acted in accord with what we placed into our hearts and conscience. Now our conscience is clear. The Bible tells us that we "…must keep hold of the deep truths of the faith with a clear conscience" (1 Timothy 3:9). So even those who speak ill of us, will later recognize that they slandered themselves. They will become ashamed (1 Peter 3:16).

We should know that our conscience differs today from its reactions yesterday. For if we have been seeking our Lord continually, we would be growing in His knowledge and faith, over the years. Thus, we have been perfecting our conscience. For this increase in knowledge and faith in God changes the values against which our thoughts and actions are judged.

So we must not only lay up God's word in our hearts and souls. We must read it regularly, reflect upon it, and meditate upon it, as says the Holy Bible. In so doing, the Word of God would become real to us and become a part of our entire being and as part of how we act and how we make choices in our lives. Thus from our very thoughts, beliefs, actions and reactions, will cause a stir of our God-like or Christ-like value system.

Conscience is living and conscious. It possesses the quality or attribute of awareness. We know that conscience warns and causes guilt, regret, torment, or approval. This means that conscience is both sensitive and responsive. Thus when we are about to take some action or even think of some deed that contradicts our standards or values, our conscience immediately warns or prompts us that what we are about to do is wrong. We may feel bad concomitant with our wrong thought or perspective action. If we persist and ignore such promptings and we continue our actions, we experience a sense of guilt. Following this, we may fully realize the negative repercussions and outcomes for which we experience regret. Were we obedient and yielded to the promptings of our conscience, we would have experienced a sense of approval and inward relief which is an indication by conscience that we have done the correct thing.

As stated, if we are about to act in violation of our morals and ethics, our conscience readily recognizes what we are about to do. It immediately receives the impressions of our intention and places it against its moral—knowledge bank for assessment. A judgment is made that our intention is in disharmony with the philosophical and moral contents of our conscience, and then we feel guilty. This is a warning signal which makes us feel ashamed and we lose face in the presence of others. It does not matter if others are aware of our intentions or not; after all, unless they are mind readers, they would not have a clue to what is transpiring in our hearts and minds. Therefore, what is important is the inward perception that our innerselves have: "we are about to violate values that are important to ourselves." We are hence judged by ourselves or our own consciences as guilty. We experience all associated emotions as inner shame, a removal of any pride, and a subconscious readiness to be penalized as a just compensation for our action or intent. Since we had not as yet committed an action, for we have had only an intent, all these associated feelings with guilt, constitute a warning or prompting telling us to desist from carrying out our intention.

If we ignore these warnings, if we act with disobedience, and continue to carry out our intentions, we receive another kind of signal from our conscience: the feelings of regret. Surely regret does not come until after the completed action. But throughout our wrong doing, we continually sense and know that guilt warning still alerting us to stop. Since the consequence of wrong is creating pain and hurt for others and always ourselves, regret is our natural resultant feeling. It is not as if conscience is a predictor of the future or godlike in knowing the outcome of our actions; rather, conscience is very mechanical here as it is operating in accordance to its moral content and values. We then become despondent with our regret. We are overcome by sadness and often review our actions with the thoughts that we should not have done it. But what is done is done. This the attitude many take to find some kind of emotional and mental peace of mind and to remove perturbed feelings—the nag of regret or the torment of conscience. But we cannot so easily sidestep our past. It will always haunt us at propitious and as 'familiar old times' recurs. Satan will make sure of this.

Our conscience is proactive when we feel guilty; and reactive when we have regrets. It is therefore a matrix of sensitivity, responsivity, and intelligence. The process of assessing our intent, and then acting to learn if they are right or wrong is an intelligible one. Guilt, regret, torment, and approval are emotions that objectify the activities of conscience. I do not know of anyone who has identified the specific location of the conscience in our bodies. Yet it seems universally accepted that everyone has a conscience. It is a self-evident reality. In mystical, philosophical, and religious writings and discussions, the conscience has always been in some way related to our hearts. In fact, in some writings the heart is used as a synonym for conscience. In the Old Testament there are several references to heart used as conscience. Perhaps, it is for this reason, in all romantic language the heart is viewed as the organ of "love." After all, the heart is the hub of our lives. To use it as an analogy for love or conscience is indicative of the importance we place on these two.

The conscience also has a key value in the moral world. For who can live properly without a good conscience? When we are wrong and guilty, the heart would be uneasy and beat faster. When we are right, our heart is relaxed and there is no anxiety. It simply beats slowly and rhythmically. It would seem that we cannot live without this conscience as much as we cannot live without the heart. The two seem to work hand in hand. One, the heart, physically and objectively indicates the state of the other, conscience. Everything we think, say, or do is evaluated as right or wrong and somewhere in between. How well we live depends on how often we act in accord with our consciences. It is popular to hear one say, "at least my conscience is clear." This is an attempt to exonerate oneself. It is a kind of self judgment and vindication—"I am not guilty," declares the innerself.

When we are about to act or decide, our internal watchman awakes. It then silently prompts us to continue or to stop. Here is the work of our conscience as an inner guardian. It stands ever alert at the doorways of our lives. We may not know exactly how it is shaped or where in our bodies it is located, but what we do know is that this conscience of ours, exists and it is real. It is a bit of digression here to say we are implying another kind of reality—one that does not consist of any kind of substance. But putting philosophical discussion aside, no one denies the existence of conscience. We speak of weak, strong, clear or seared consciences. We know our conscience is permanently employed. It always knows, it never sleeps. It is a twenty-four hour security system. It is preventative and solution-oriented.

Think of a computerized banking machine. As soon as we insert our bankcard, the machine or rather the electronic device is ready to go. It is alerted. But no reaction follows from the device until that point when we indicate our intended action. The device remains on the alert until we punch in our private code. Here, it then recognizes the code as us. It asks us what we want to do: withdraw, deposit, transfer, or check our balances? The device, still being alert, then asks us to be clear and specific; for example, how much do we want to withdraw? We key in the amount and it comes out with a recorded action and account balance. This process of first placing requests against our account; then secondly, calculating and displaying the outstanding balance while still being alert for further banking transactions, describes the activity of our conscience.

Our conscience acts as a measuring rod, as a kind of yardstick with standards as the divisional units. Our intentions, words, and actions are put against this conscious, judging rod to conclude if they are acceptable or not.

As with a security system, once the electronic contact brakes, an alarm goes off and lights begin to flash. So it is with conscience. Once the measuring process ends, and the decision is that a thought, intention, word, or action is accepted or rejected by our inner watchman and judge, we receive a signal or an alarm in the form of a feeling of guilt, regret, torment, or approval.

Conscience, we have said, works in conjunction with our bodies. Any condition that is in harmony with our bodily or health system, we feel pleasure or no discomfort. When however such a condition is out of harmony with our bodies or health, we feel pain or discomfort. The emotions of pleasure and pain tell us whether or not conditions are harmonious to ourselves. Our conscience also uses this emotional meter as well and its readings are in the form of guilt, regret, torment, or approval. Let us point out that approval can simply be a sense of peace or inner calm. This is pleasurable or a no-pain state or experience.

We often say that conscience must guide us. This gives the impression that our conscience can decide what we must do in specific situations. But this is untrue. Conscience guides us only in the sense that it warns or advises us if our actions are consistent or not with the morals we have established in our hearts. We may compare the guidance of conscience with the sonar of submarines or with the radar of aeroplanes. I am not a pilot or aeronautical engineer, but these instruments do not dictate which direction the "carrier" should go; rather, they assist the pilots to steer effectively by providing valuable information about the path or journey.

What if our morals are wrong or our establishing them is wrong, then obviously our conscience would not be standing on solid ground. We would not be able to depend on our conscience nor would we be able to argue convincingly with others that we are right. There are other questionable issues that we will discus later, like what is right and wrong for you may not be right and wrong for me and so on. Here is a start of relative versus universal or absolute morals.

When we are warned, we know to stop our current course of action or intention. When we feel regret, we know to apologize, if applicable, and then redo or correct what we have said or done. What happens to a person who has a seared conscience? Here we show some presumption on our part in our perception and value of the morality of another. But from a Biblical standpoint, or rather, from the Christian Bible standpoint, there is a universal or absolute value system: God's Word. The person with a seared conscience, we have seen often, suddenly feels guilty over a wrongful action which he would not have normally given a second thought. From where did this sudden virtuous impulse come? And why did it choose the time it did? The Bible says that Christ wants to save everyone. He wants us all to have the knowledge of truth (1 Timothy 2:3). Therefore, He is patient and tolerant with us; for despite our sinful nature, our Lord still by his Holy Spirit convicts us and always seeks to have us turn and do the right thing.

When persons with hearts of stone become tired of their evil ways as happiness of this kind is only temporary, their spirits still cry out in the wilderness for salvation and to be flooded by God's love. For even the vilest, when in pain, screams and shouts "O God." It is like an automatic, universal, response or calling-out beyond to **The Authority** with ultimate power who we know inwardly can help. It is like an inherent part of all humans—no matter their race nor creed.

Then when the person shouts, "Why me? Why must this happen to me?" This desperate questioning implies the expectation of an answer. But from whom must this answer come when we scream in privacy? For when all else has failed: as we have talked with friends, specialists, and ourselves—using reason and intelligence, then our desperate outcries are not simply a physical scream to let out our emotional pressures; but that someone, anyone else will hear us and come up with an answer. There is no one else except the idea of God: an invisible Mind Force that is universal, all-knowing, everywhere, and almighty.

But at this point of weakness, this point of total and absolute defeat we face our inadequacy and the folly of our personal vanity. The defeat of the pride in our hearts, the defeat of our presumptuous, self-opinionated personalities is the condition that is perfect for the entering of our Lord and the guidance of His Holy Spirit. This is the point wherein all the emotions associated with a yielding, submissive and dependent spirit are active. Our hearts are ready and receptive to be scolded. We are on the brink of hopefulness; we are at the breaking point prior to the moment of an upward movement. It is the true moment of change for the better. God is ever ready to pull us up and out of our selfish, pitiless, evil hole we dug for ourselves. Here is the moment of truth, the point of readiness to receive Christ, the critical time of rebirth, and the *old man* is dead and the *new man* is born. We are in the body of Christ Consciousness; we are his obedient sons and daughters.

We must remember Christ said to Nicodemus that "…no one can see the kingdom of God unless he is born again" (John 3:3). To the Orthodox Christian this text does not refer to the doctrine of reincarnation, but to others it does. The Biblical position is clear with respect to reincarnation. The Bible says, "Just as man is destined to die once, and after that to face judgement" (Heb. 9:27). However, the correct exegesis to John 3:3 is not the issue here. In both interpretations (single or many lives), individuals are encouraged to seek such values which most certainly must be pure, highly spiritual, and Christlike. Christ further told the disciples they must humble themselves like a child to inherit the kingdom of God along with its blessings (Matthew 18:1-4). Clearly such humility constitutes a yielding and submission to the Will and Wishes of God: hence obedience to Universal or Divine promptings. The desperate person with a seared conscience is at that point where he is helpless, and cannot find any solutions. It is there and then his "noisy," evil self is silent and he can hear the whisperings of the Holy Spirit (Psalm 4:4). Still, he has free will and may so choose to disobey and continue to self destruction.

Surely, his evil companions will think that he has gone soft. Not being facetious, but if they are correct, then he is blessed. For being soft is the condition of the heart in which the Holy Ghost requires to work—one that is in complete surrender. It is not that the Holy Spirit had stopped prompting the right actions to the vile person; rather, such an individual chose to ignore the promptings when they heard them. In the midst and heights of pride, Satan makes evil sweet, beautiful, insatiable, and indelible. The vile mind succeeds and enjoys the perverted pleasure of deeds. Having a seared conscience is like being drugged or drunken and in such a state, one has false perceptions of realities. Hence lies become truths for convenience and any kind of evil action is justified pleasurably.

Let it be known that a soft and charitable heart is one that is contrite and made supreme. It is a Christ-like heart. Its softness generates compassion and love. It alludes to the gentility of Christ, the forgiveness of God, and the comforting of His Holy Spirit. To be soft is to be ready for spirituality, to be obedient to the directives of the Holy Spirit, is to be in tune with the pain God feels, and to be sensitive to the hurts of humanity.

Who can go before an inquisitor, accused of a crime he did not commit, and refuses to defend himself—knowing that if found guilty, his death will be slow and excruciating? Perhaps a few of us. But among this few, name an individual who will accept blame for the wrong doings of all humans and who would accept the ultimate sentence of torture, insults, false accusations, and death?

The Christian Bible tells us there was one such man: Jesus the Christ. We learn, too, there was a record of many non-violent men and women who suffered severely for their ideas and ideals. Some even lost their lives—the Christian martyrs.

But none carried "the cross of burdens" on their shoulders for the world except the Christ. Nevertheless, we must recognize that all self-sacrificing individuals are exceedingly strong willed; that they too are Christlike; that their spirits are in oneness with the Spirit of God; and that they have strong consciences. No matter the extent of their sacrifices, they always put the glory of God and the benefit of humanity before their own lives. They are neither mad, nor foolish. But if they were, then their madness is music in the heart of God and their folly to God is wisdom. For is that not how we classify men and women with altruistic purposes? When they glorify God and give up their riches to others for nothing in return, we call them fools; and when they martyred themselves for not denying Christ, we say they are mad. The state or nature of our consciences—weak, strong, clear, or seared—becomes the law of our being. It drives us, stirs us, and ruffles us even when we appear to be calm to ensure our intentions, thoughts, and acts are in harmony with who we really are.

The Need to Read

If we must satisfy our needs in general for our psychological or spiritual stability and our physical harmony; then we must understand what they are, how they came about, and their requirements for fulfilment. Take reading for instance. Is it not a need but something we wilfully do and which we may or may not enjoy? But its pleasure or displeasure we are not concern with now. Reading is an act that is driven. Almost everyone does it. It can be habitual; it becomes second nature with practice. It is almost compulsory for community, for society, for life. For rules, laws, procedures, and jokes are all written. Reading is an experience. When we read, our intellect is reading with words, images outside ourselves to produce meaning and understanding. Reading is therefore purposeful.

To read, it is self-evident that we use our eyes, brain, and mind, or in the case of blind persons, they use their fingers, brain, and mind. Whichever method we use, reading involves the recognition of words so connected in our language forming sentences, paragraphs, and having specific meanings—or at least the reader's interpretation of what is read. In other words, reading is more effectual in comparison with needs, which are more causal. When combined, however, "The Need To Read" is the impetus to cast our eyes on or explore information for knowledge, pleasure or entertainment. Its results at best, is a contribution to our inner growth—an understanding of something now, a clearer and broader view, a lessening of the heaviness of our hearts through entertainment.

Reading provides a form of fulfilment. It must therefore give our inner being some elements necessary for our existence. After all, the one thing we can be sure of is that we all are ever changing. Hopefully, this means we are always growing upwards and onwards—becoming better people. Supposedly everything we do contributes to our becoming better persons or closer to the point of who we are expected to be while here incarnate in the physical bodies of ours. I know this statement is fatalistic, so let me change it to include the idea that reading contributes to our becoming more awakened or evolved soul personalities.

To the religious then, we will become more Christlike or true imitators of the Christ we emulate. It is incontestable that many of our experiences seem to send us along a downward path. This happens when we decide on options in life that take us to a point society perceives as "backwards." We may need this so-called, perceptual backwardness or devolution before we can begin to go forward. We congratulate writers and historians who documented the past. To these historical events, we can refer and learn from the pitfalls of our past generations. No one on this point can argue against the value to read and the need for this ability. To the neophyte or milk drinker (1 Pet. 2:2; Heb. 5:12, 13) these experiences are novel and uplifting; to the meat eaters or matured postulants (Heb. 5:14), these experiences are confirmations of what they are already adept at.

It is obviously unwise for us to presume and negatively ascribe any individual's experience as backwards. As individuals, we take our own path. Once we acquire some kind of knowledge that move us closer to profound peace, we cannot discredit another's experience. We have learned that "one [person's] meat is another [person's] poison"?

Before we discuss how reading contributes to the evolution of our personality, we must talk about the difference between needs and desires. We confuse them in speech. We use them as synonyms. They are not. There is a thin and almost invisible line separating them. This distinction is not important enough for some. In a Marketing course, for instance, I have listened to my university lecturer used these words interchangeably. There was the same interchanging use of the words "desire" and "need" in the textbook prescribed for the course. A customer's need, writes the authors, for a product or service, is same as having a desire for it—or so presumes marketing. For this course, needs and wants were the same. After all, the business person is not investing in a moral venture; but rather in a profitable one. The semantic distinction between needs and wants are not important enough for our investors—they are given exact weights or values.

For it is true that whether I desire or need the product or service, I am plagued by a subconscious motivation to have it. It is upon this fact that marketing is based. Marketing does not concern itself with the exact meaning of the words desire and need. No businessperson is concerned with semantics on this point. Neither can we find fault against a businessperson on this question. What matters, regardless of the meanings of these words, is if the potential buyer possesses a strong enough motive (desire or need) to pay for the product or service. This motive the businessperson is happy to identify. After having done so, it justifies production, manufacture, distribution, and sales. Motive is the seed of profits—the starting point towards the "Nirvana" or success of the business world.

How are the meanings of these words—desire and need— important to our discussion on "reading in relations to conscience"? What value is reading to our conscience anyway? How can knowledge gained from this exercise help us? First we said, a desire or a want is an active principle. It is present in our minds, positively reaching out for fulfilment. It seems unstable by itself. It is always seeking to be complete. It reminds us of certain chemical substances that are unstable in their original state of existence and must therefore seek out another with which it must combine and be stable.

As an illustration, we learn in Grade 12 Chemistry class that the oxygen (O) atom is one and must combine with another becoming (O_2) the chemist tells us. The one (O) by itself is unstable; it requires another—becoming (O_2) to be stable. This principle, or some may say mystical law, likewise applies to every kind of need or desire. When we desire an object or condition, our inner selves will know when we get it. For our desires are unstable and cannot exist by themselves *ad infinitum*—without end. They are constantly seeking satisfaction. They are so polemically positive and aggressive; we can say they are our main *drives* lodged in the centre of our attention. I am not a psychologist, but when we desire something, we often seem to have a definite idea what that "something" is; that is, at least the properties of the 'something' that would give us a state of calm and create a condition of harmonium for which our desire clamours.

A girlfriend, in a discussion on needs and desires, said, "When a woman desires to look beautiful, she develops the need for specific beauty products like clothes, makeup, face cream, and so on. Then she goes shopping because she feels she must have these products. Of course this is one girl's perception of beauty. It is an external, physical, and materialistic view. There is of course the psychological, the more spiritual, and the inner perception which experience tells us operates similarly. For instance, the desire for a more profound and spiritual lifestyle may stir us to read more religious or mystical books. It may cause us to find time to reflect and meditate so we may raise our inner consciousness to a higher level. If these examples are true, what causes these desires? How do they come into being?

The desire to look beautiful, for example, implies unhappiness with oneself or dissatisfaction, at least. The person's self perception, regardless of what stimulated it (advertisements, new values, or whatever), is on the downside. Although we merely want to improve our looks, we still imply dissatisfaction with our existing self image. This means that based on our standards for measuring beauty, we judged ourselves to be substandard. This gap between how we see ourselves and our determination of good-looks causes our low self esteem. This gap described is what we must bridge to feel self confident and have a positive self image. The intent to bridge this gap is our goal. This intent drives us, pushes like a force for the quality or element that will give us fulfilment. This intent is what we call desire. The gap then, is our need. If therefore we were to change our value of beauty to agree with our self perception, then we will no longer have our self esteem problem. At this point we will be content with ourselves. We will have achieved self acceptance; that is, fulfilment and satisfaction. Thus the related desire and need become nonexistent.

No matter our desire or want, it is set off by a need. For instance, when we want or desire water, it is because we are thirsty, or we are experiencing a small degree of dehydration, or our taste for it has been activated. Similarly, the desire for food may imply hunger or some condition requiring the nutrients or elements from what we will eat. Sometimes too the desire is awakened by habit. For in this instance, we remember the smell and have sensual recognition of the food which we know in our memory what it will do to us—give us satisfaction—we are driven or develop the desire for it. Thus it may be that the benefits and pleasure we derive from food has been stimulated. These desires are propelled and originated from a need for the condition that will cause satisfaction. What is important to remember, and we reemphasize it here, is that all desires appear to be driven by some obvious or subconscious need.

A need, on the other hand, is passive. It is like a negative state that sits and awaits fulfilment, unlike a desire that seems to go after a condition of stability. Both need and desire are incomplete—both must have another item, thing, or condition to stabilize them. Both appear to travel the same route—desire, however, seem to be ahead of need and closer to arriving at its destination or point of stability. No wonder their distinction matters little to the business person. It would seem that need, desire, and satisfaction are the triune elements of a stable condition—each being a stage in the fulfilment of the law of the Triangle. The business goal is the provision of a product or service that will satisfy the potential customer possessing the need or better— the desire.

Additionally, desire is often open to alternative means or objects of satisfaction. It in itself is not seeking satisfaction. But it seeks the condition that will marry or blend with the need behind it. Without need, desires are nonexistent. Desire, therefore, is like a product of an antecedent need which propels the desire to move and reach for fulfilment. This point we commonly call satisfaction. So the need to read is not the same as the desire to read. The "need to read" will refer to a state of lack or "a general kind of emptiness for the benefits of information." Whereas a "desire to read" will refer to a decisive hunt to peruse data by going to libraries, bookstores, the internet and wherever one may acquire reading materials. We can visualise that one with a need sitting lazily and basking in a euphoria of wishful thinking and imagining. While a person with the desire is up and around knocking doors and beating the streets and shops and bookshelves and computers for what he or she seeks.

The aphorism "I have hidden your word in my heart that I might not sin against you" (Psalm 119:11) is probably one of the greatest truths by which humans must live to succeed in both their physical and spiritual affairs. For if God's word is in our hearts and souls, if we keep it there by regularly reading, reflecting, and meditating upon it; then in the times that we need it, it will be there for us in the fore front of our minds and thoughts, actively fulfilling His promise of deliverance. Here we can realise by the implication of ourselves having the need of God's deliverance and the fulfilment of His promises in our lives as we assess ourselves of not having these God given blessings. Here too we see that if we actively desire God gifts and blessings of deliverance, then we must read and place His Words into our hearts and minds so that when we need them in our lives, they are ever present and automatic.

The Bible tells us that even our Lord Jesus laid up the word of His Father in His heart and soul. For when Satan tried to influence Him to disobey God, Jesus said to Satan, "It is written: Man does not live on bread alone, but on every word that comes from the mouth of God" (Matthew 4:4). Clearly, our Lord Jesus, the ultimate in character example, read the scriptures. Why else would he state "It is written…" unless he was aware by reading that his statement is fact? He has illustrated in many other instances in the Bible His familiarity with the Holy Scriptures.

Further, He showed that one of the main values of reading the scriptures is the assurance and confirmation of divine truths and realities. When John the Baptist sent his disciples on an errand to find out if Jesus was the One expected, the saviour of the world;

Jesus told them "Go back and report to John what you hear and see: the blind receive sight, the lame walk, those who have leprosy are cured, the deaf hear, the dead are raised, and the good news is preached to the poor. Blessed is the man who does not fall away on account of me" (Matthew 11:2-6). These things were written prophesies indicating they will be done by the Lamb of God, by humanity's Redeemer (Isaiah 35:4-6). Moreover, Jesus' statement clearly tells us that he knew that John must have read the Scriptures as well.

If John did not read the scriptures himself, he probably would have died not knowing that he had fulfilled his mission in preparing the way for the One who would baptize repenters in the spirit. But Jesus was sure that John was indeed conversant with the Holy Scriptures and its prophesies. For what other reason would He have quoted them?

The value of reading cannot be overemphasized. Those who say they are too busy; their chores are too time consuming; they cannot spare their free moments; or they have better ways to use their time, lack the charm of character and the gentility that reading engenders. As the more we read the more we learn. Thus we realize the largeness of our own ignorance—the vast amount of knowledge we do not have. I am not saying that by reading we realize how foolish we are; rather, we discover how little we know and we are overwhelmed by how much we can learn.

Can individuals really absorb the knowledge they need in their lives' span? Or would the balance be added to what they have learned in this incarnation, when they enter the kingdom of God? Is the acquirement of divine knowledge our purpose on earth? Solomon said that we should "Fear God and keep His commandments, for this is the whole duty of man" (Ecclesiastes 12:13). We dare not doubt Solomon's wisdom, for we know that God gave it to him. God has said, "I will give you a wise and discerning heart, so that there will never have been anyone like you nor will there ever be" (1 Kings 3:12).

If we are to carry out God's commandments, needless to say, we must know what they are. Hence we must read, study, and apply them (Psalm 119:97-104). I cannot understand churchgoers who claim to love God and know they must obey him and still who would refuse to read His Words. They depend on the Sunday sermons and rely on the homiletics of the pastors and priests. Whether or not we become familiar with all God's divine laws in this life, our duty is become familiar with them and to keep on obeying His commands. For we will only inherit what He has promised or attain profound peace if we obey what He says (Deuteronomy 4:1-2). In this regard, a dire conviction and support for reincarnation, regeneration, or any fatalistic view of rebirth is irrelevant.

Reading also brings us pleasure. Keep in mind we are here to focus on God's word (Psalm 119:103). Even with other books, when we simply dwell on the thoughts of what we read; if we assume the experience told and described; if we put ourselves in the story and experience the joys and sorrows, the successes and failures; this practice can be fulfilling. Such experiences help us to become closer to some of life's truths and embrace those realities that we might not have encountered on our personal path to God. Hence our experience and knowledge is enriched with such gems of wisdom which can only bring a greater and fuller realization of the wonderful mysteries of life. 'Ah Sweet Mysteries of Life,' would be the sighs of the mystics and some illumined or spiritually enlightened souls.

Seeing a situation or condition through the eyes of others when they tell us their stories, helps to sharpen our perceptions and broaden our visions. We no longer remain narrow-minded. We become tolerant of someone else's differences instead of creating dissentions, arguments, and even war. Being objective, having an open mind, and seeing things from another's viewpoint, prepares us for brotherly kindliness (2 Peter 1:7) and being our brother's keeper (Romans 12:10, 16). We learn to appreciate how they feel and what they like. We become respectful of what they value. It develops fair-mindedness too.

Reading expands our knowledge base. Many persons may argue that we can only have true knowledge from experience; that is, having an intimate interaction between our personal consciousness and facts or actualities. They may further contend that in reading we are not actually and personally experiencing anything; but passively perusing someone else's thoughts and realities. Such a suggestion is partly true; but we cannot deny that in reading, there is the presence or existence of intellectual and emotional activities as reflection, understanding, interpretation, perception, memorizing, imaging, appreciating, visualizing, and even daydreaming.

Mystically speaking, the interaction between our consciousness and actualities is on three different levels. One is the material or the objective; the other, the subjective; and the last is the spiritual.

On the objective level, we are concerned with our physical senses and its associated pain-pleasure sensations which signals whether the experience is undesirable or desirable. Psychology tells us that what we see, hear, or touch for instance, we do with our physical or objective consciousness. This means that impulses from outside of ourselves impact on our consciousness to produce sensations. When different impulses unite with our awareness, we have various sensations—each sensation will constitute an item or point of knowledge or fact.

On the subjective level, our experiences are more mental or intellectual—having to deal to a greater degree with our thoughts and ideas. According to students of mysticism, the divine law is fulfilled; that is, consciousness plus actualities give personal experiences from which knowledge is derived. Within this subjective level is where reading mostly belongs. Physics teaches us that the impulses created by the light vibrations, reflected by the words, are interpreted by our minds. We learn this in grade 12 physics. This interpretation and recognition ultimately fill our memory with knowledge gained through subjective experience.

According to the Bible, when we, however, "lay up" the words, the Biblical values, the thoughts, the ideas, and the examples in our hearts; when we reflect on them, meditate on them, and then ask our Lord Jesus to let, as He has promised, His Holy Spirit give us the understanding—His understanding, we are in reality formulating judgmental standards for our conscience. I am not saying that the whisperings from the Holy Spirit, that Divine Intelligence of God, is the same as the voice from the conscience. I am saying that when we communicate with God, we benefit bountifully as we complied with His edict, "Be still, and know that I am God" (Psalm 46:10). What we receive, we add to the functional moral base that our conscience use.

Communication is a two-way process. We must also at times stop our active petitioning in prayer and listen in respectful and humble silence to our Lord as He blesses us with His Presence and begins to whisper to us such divine and golden secrets for true success. These whisperings, these spiritual promptings, these inspirational thoughts and ideas, constitute the realization, and fulfilment of the Law on the spiritual and subliminal level—consciousness plus actualities gives personal experience then knowledge. This is truly the process of meditation upon the word of God. It is a kind of reading in which we attempt to reconnect with the mind and heart of God at the time His Words were formed in the one He used to write the specific scripture. What did the writer feel at that time? What were his expectations then? What was the context and thus, the true meaning or principle?

Herein His Holy Spirit talks to us and gives us the understanding of the scriptures. These spiritual truths are the values and standards we place in our hearts, in our souls. These, along with the objective realities: those truths on the material, mundane level that are sound and are in harmony with God's word and laws, all comprise the authoritative library of our personal judge and inner guardian, our conscience.

The Bible says, if we lay up God's word in our hearts and souls and if we reflect on it, meditate on it regularly, it will prevent us from committing sin. Here is how our conscience truly guides us, by warning us that what we are thinking or doing or intend to do is wrong. The promptings of "don't do" or "do" is our conscience in action. This true master within us, we can depend on only when we flood our thoughts and life with the "blood of Christ;" when we dwell and live in His consciousness and abide in Him. Christ says, "Remain in me, and I will remain in you. No branch can bear fruit by itself…If you remain in me and my words remain in you, ask whatever you wish, and it will be given you" (John 14:4,7).

We can be certain, as he has promised, that our petition will be answered when we submit to the will of Almighty God, by letting His words become alive in our lives. For He has said, "Have faith in God,…whatever you ask for in prayer, believe that you have received it, and it will be yours" (Mark 11:22-24).

We absolutely need to read—whether we want to or not. For how else can we hope to have eternal life. The Bible says that we will be destroyed because of our ignorance (Hosea 4:6). Reading is a major means of learning and of knowing—of removing ignorance. By reading rightly, by putting God's words in our hearts, in our souls, in our conscience, we are ensuring that our word is God's.

The Power to Choose

There are many scriptures in the Holy Bible that tell us that God has given each one of us free will and the power to choose. The doctrine of predestination or election, does not take away our abilities as individuals to choose freely. King Saul, for instance, was appointed by God to rule over God's people; but it was his free choice to sin and disobey God that caused him to lose his kingdom to David. It was Saul's disobedience that caused God to remove His Holy Spirit from him. Similarly, it was Adam and Eve's decision to wrongly exercise their free will and disobey God. As a result, they were removed from the blessed paradise—the garden of Eden.

Thus it is this same free will, which is good but wrongly applied, that was responsible for humanity being separated from God. Freedom of religious belief, for instance, is a constitutional right for every person in a free and democratic society like Canada. One Canadian lawyer, on behalf of his client, argued in the courts of appeal: "No matter my client's right or wrong interpretation of a biblical verse, there is enough evidence that my client has demonstrated his sincerity of belief. Therefore, to deny him exemption on the grounds of religious belief under the law, is an infringement of his right to religious freedom." We use our free will to fight for rights and benefits—though our beliefs are not always credible and may be a result of exegetical and hermeneutical fallacies. So it is still our free will that corrupts us. It is this same free will that brought evil into the world—Satan did not create evil.

Today, our life experiences also give us several testimonies to the truth of humanity's endowment of the freedom to choose. No matter the type of political society in which we live, this freedom exists. It is true that some governmental policies and laws may be so enforced as to curtail this natural human freedom. But it is the decision and "free choice" of the oppressed citizenry to comply with such oppression. For they can use their free will, as many have in the past and some are in the present, to rebel.

God has also provided us with both natural and spiritual laws; and He has given us the free will to obey these laws. For He created us to love and worship Him. But He did not—even in His election—use force to receive our love and worship. So with the freedom He gave us, we can also disobey Him. If we comply with His laws and obey Him, everlasting life is ours; if we do otherwise, we reap eternal damnation and contempt. Needless to say, we are tormented by our consciences when we disobey; and there is this feeling of inner peace or of "weightlessness"; that is, no burden in our hearts, when we obey.

The theme of blessings and curses runs throughout the Bible and is a fact of life. After all, the Bible is The Living Word. It is God's Word and He is alive and He is eternal. Even those who support the predestination philosophy—stating that all human life is preordained—will agree that the reward and punishment system is a universal and divine one. Look at King David, who was loved by the Lord, the Bible tells us. He violated the commands of God and committed adultery. He chose to abuse his position of authority to seduce Uriah's wife, Bathsheba (2 Sam. 11:2-5). After she became pregnant, David unjustly ordered Uriah's death to publicly make her his wife (2 Sam. 11:14-17). But this child they conceived in adultery was taken by the Lord. However, God spared their lives. Though King David, a man after God's own heart, sought in prayer and fasting, forgiveness for his action and life of his child God's judgement was evident. God is consistent and fair. He punishes the sin and not the sinner (Ps. 89:31-33).

Life is activity. Each of which is evaluated by its pleasure-pain outcomes. If painful, we are cursed; if pleasurable, we are blessed. When there is no pain nor pleasure, but just a peace of mind, then that too, constitute pleasure. For pain signals when something is wrong, when some condition is out of harmony with the law of the situation. Thus if there is no pain, but peace and calm, we posit there must be harmonium. There was no sinful activity. It is obviously a condition for which we should celebrate in a manner of our choosing.

But our God is more compassionate and practical and would not only wait to compensate us after we die or pass through transition. He blesses us now, in this life, when we obey Him (Gen. 12). We realise some benefits now, in today's world and on this earthly realm when we comply with His laws and wishes. He releases riches to us. He opens doors of opportunities for our betterment, grants us good health as well as healings of our ailments—physical, mental, emotional and spiritual. Similarly, we pay now for those times we disobey Him. The curses come along with the blessings—now or later.

But presently we are not concerned with free will in relation to our earning eternal life. Rather, we are going to stay within the bounds of this incarnation; that is, the use of free will and choice through maturity until our earthly death or transition. We are therefore looking at how our conscience responds to our thoughts and actions as we live now.

The question we must address is what part does our free will play in the operations of our conscience? To put it another way, how does the exercising of our power to choose affect the sensitivity and responsivity of our conscience? But what is this power to choose anyway? And what is free will? Are they one and the same? Do we have any power at all? Or is this so-called power in fact our ability to allow ourselves to be used by God; that is, our letting ourselves yield to His will and wishes? Does this power refer to a kind of capability to motivate "self" to initiate certain kinds of actions which may actuate or set in motion the laws of nature?

"Power to choose" refers to man's freedom to select "A" instead of "B." This freedom means allowance or permission granted. It infers there is no absolute obstruction, if any, to stop an election. Further, the intellect of the chooser can be applied—using logic, reason and analysis—to facilitate the choice. It also implies a conditional want; that is, an element that would fulfil some implicit need. But more than this, choice indicates that more than one element exist which can fulfil the need. The final choice represents the incumbent's preference, after comparisons and critical thinking are done prior to the actual resultant election. Since power refers to capability. We may conclude the chooser has a *natural and divine right* to exercise his or her choice.

We note that will and choice are dissimilar. Choice is a decision after considering alternatives. It is the exercising of one's preferences. Will is an activity principle. It is not a force. As soon as we place some wish or specific determination at the focus of our attention, we activate will. It is obedient to our focused desires. For example, if we choose an apple instead of an orange from a table, the apple is first our preference or decision; the act of taking it and physically touching or moving it shows it is our choice. *Choice is the objectification, the materialization of a decision*. That "something" which causes our desire to become or to transform into a *realised* preference or choice is our will.

As stated, freedom or free will is allowance, it is permission. We often think of free will in context with our individual desires, whims or fancies. If we have an affinity to an object, nothing or no one can normally stop us from trying to draw closer to the object. Our will characterises our ability to achieve whatever appeals to us. Will is therefore causal. And desire is its impetus. When we have a need and the free will to fulfil it, it is desire that drives us towards satisfaction. Once we have found the element of fulfilment or the subject sought, a choice is made. It is this exercised choice that actuates conscience.

"The power to choose is probably the greatest blessing given to [humans] by God," says one writer and public speaker. Many will agree with him because most life experiences are caused by our active or passive choice. However, there are those who feel that the life and vitality called Christ is humanity's greatest gift from God (John 3:16). For the Bible tells us to imitate Christ and to yoke ourselves with him or abide in him (Matt. 11:29; Col. 3:3; Jn. 15:7).

Choice is the reason for our birth and entry into the world. Even when it seems accidental or unplanned, a choice was made by someone. It may have been at the wrong moment or in an untimely manner and place; nevertheless, it was started by someone's premature choosing. An accident implies an occurrence about which we have no foreknowledge. Once it turns out positive, we may assume it to be possibly caused by divine intervention. Whatever the incident or outcome, it began with someone choosing.

Power is the ability to cause or to bring into effect. It also implies authority. We are, however, concerned with the former meaning now. Power is a kind of potential force or energy at rest. Like the basin of a reservoir, just waiting for the trap doors to be removed and so release this enormous flow of water that produces electricity, when this latent kind of power is released, it becomes activated and causal and affects whatever stands in its way.

Choice is the act of wilfully taking one thing instead of another. It suggests a process of selection in which an examination of options was conducted. Comparisons are then made and the best option taken. This option constitutes a choice.

Man's power to choose is his capability to voluntarily bring any condition he feels or desires into existence, or to accept or reject one thing instead of another. For analogy, we may choose to attend the University of Toronto instead of any other in the world; or we may choose to belong to a political party, a mystical organization, or a particular church or religion instead of any other that exists.

The premise upon which choice is based, presupposes that we are all free agents and can thus determine our own destinies: directions, goals, ideals. In the Holy Scriptures, God told Moses, "This day I call heaven and earth as witnesses against you that I have set before you life and death, blessings and curses" Now choose life, so that you and your children may live" (Deut. 30:19). Clearly God informed Moses of his options and went beyond to recommend the better choice. I am not now joining the debate on the overworked topic of free will versus predestination in regards to man's final judgment. I leave that to the Augustinian and Calvinists to battle with the Armenian and John Wesley's followers.

The evidence is overwhelming that humans do have the God given right to choose and to determine their own future on earth. Clearly, if we analyze our present professions, occupations, memberships, and involvements, we come to realize that they are the results of our choices. It is these choices that are responsible for our happiness and sadness in life. It is these choices that bring us the successes and failures we experience. It is these choices that motivate us, that encourage us, and that cause us to do and not to do things. It is these choices that govern our lives and point out the directions in which we eventually go.

Everyone chooses the things and situations that please them. And since choosing is always between two or among a number of items or things, such choices are more appropriately called preferences. In other words, we may choose "A" instead of "B." We may therefore say we prefer "A" to "B." Further, to choose "A," means that the qualities of "A" give us more pleasure or find greater harmony with our personalities. This harmony is as a result of the blending of the qualities of "A" and the needs of our personalities.

There are many desires within us: the desire for more money, a better life, fame, authority, to be closer to God, to be educated and so on. These are not permanent conditions, nor are they all blessings endowed upon us by a Higher Authority. Rather, they are mostly self-created: resulting from internal and external influences. They are formed by our interaction in society through the media, conversations, and spiritual experiences.

Desires are active principles. As stated in an earlier chapter, they drive us to find satisfaction. They have much to do with our choices. In fact, when we choose one thing, in preference to another, it is because we desire the chosen thing more than the others. In other words, we have consciously made a decision that what we chose was best for us.

Naturally, such a decision must be made with the analyzing, the comparing, and the contrasting of the facts within our minds. In some instances there must be an emotional harmony caused by the blending of the desire and option. The result of these mental processes is known as our decision; and when they are objectified, we call and accept them as our choices. Such objectification may take the form of either our declaring or indicating physically that we want this or that.

This decision of ours, this choice, involves our values; that is, our morals and ethics formed from our personal and impersonal experiences in life. The wise tells us we are our thoughts. The Christian Bible tells us that "…as [we] thinketh in [our] heart, so [are we]…" (Proverbs 23:7, **KJV**). Therefore, if the qualities of "A" conform to or are in harmony with our morals and ethics, they are then acceptable to our minds. Our conscience would signal approval and we would choose "A." After all, it is natural for our personalities to want only such sensations and harmonious conditions that are pleasing to themselves.

From the above, it is clear that our way of thinking forms the basis of our actions as individuals. It must, therefore, affect the persons and situations about us. Naturally, such persons may have different conceptions and will respond differently from us to the conditions of life. This will undoubtedly cause conflict as no group can achieve its objectives when members of the same group hold different conceptions of the same objectives.

For there to be harmony with our conceptions, we must all consider the common good of the group or society of which we are a part, according to Aristotle. The Apostle Paul says, "…we are taking pains to do what is right, not only in the eyes of the Lord but also in the eyes of men" (2 Corinthians 8:21). As it was with Apostle Paul, so too we must all ensure, as much as possible, that our concepts are intended to affect those about us in a constructive way.

The question may arise that while our choices may be given to the benefit of others about us, or be such that those about us find agreement with them, they may not be in accord to the natural and spiritual laws of the universe. Consequently, such choices would not in reality benefit anyone. We know this when our conscience torments us the same time our intentions are known to our inner selves. Naturally, our assumption here is that our conscience itself is trained along universal or divine principles. But as stated above, we must do like Paul and take "pains to do what is right in the eyes of the Lord." This means training our conscience with the Holy Scriptures.

On this question of training, we find in our societies, different religions, cultures, ideologies, psychological and social pressures affect our values. This bombardment of varying impressions upon our inner selves, makes our choosing difficult. Whether or not our choices are correct or our interpretations of these impressions blend with universal principles will be difficult for us to determine. Each of us will have different interpretations for common and individual encounters and thus society will be a meeting place of conflicting views and ideas.

For the development of society, there must be some way in which we are free to think and feel as we individually want to and at the same time live harmoniously. We need to be tolerant of ideas and views that differ from our own. We can experiment in a free thinking society. We can experience and discover new ways of doing things; and learn about the complexities of life about and within us. Common sense tells us that if each person should familiarize himself with the natural and spiritual laws of the universe. Each should let his interpretations of life be in harmony with such laws, so group objectives, cooperation, and peace—call these compromises if you like—are possible.

The practice of regular, fervent praying and intense listening with humility and obedience affords each of us a personal relationship with God. In this relationship, we can all attain direct wisdom and illumination of God's rules and regulations. Such a contact is intimate and not through another individual. Therefore our experiences are direct, personal, and real. They are comprehensible to us in a language that we understand, in a form that we recognize, and in a time that is most needed.

Many of us make contacts with this all-knowing source of divine information unconsciously; we feel the presence of the Holy Spirit and do not know that we were for a moment hidden in the consciousness of Christ. We, nevertheless, benefit from the hunches and peaceful feelings which we had (Matthew 11:29)

If we follow these promptings, these subtle impellings, and use them as a backbone to our choices, we cannot fail to enjoy the true riches of life and demonstrate by our own life that the power to choose is indeed one of humanity's greatest blessings from God. Indeed, we are truly blessed for God promises that if we seek Him with all our heart we will find him (Jer. 29:13). And as believers, he says, "...I will put My law in their minds, and write it on their hearts; and I will be their God, and they shall be My people. No more shall every man teach his neighbour, and every man his brother, saying, 'Know the Lord,' for they all shall know Me..." (Jer. 31:33-34). This then is the universes Moral Law against which all our choices will be judged.

Being Where We Are

Our position in life is one of the most perplexing realities we have to face as conscious beings. We normally judge this position by time, space, and our self-perception. We study how old we are, where we live and work, what we have achieved and what we have failed. The answers to these questions we put against our conceptions of success and failure to judge ourselves. If our present position harmonizes with our conceptions, we are happy and our self-esteem is high; otherwise, we depart from the mirror of self examination with disappointment.

First, let us realize we are filled with assumptions like "with age must come reason" and this is an error. There are many biblical references that testify to this truism. For the Bible says that Josiah, son of David, was eight years old when he became king of Jerusalem; and reigned for thirty-one years. In his youth, he feared the Lord and he began to purge Judah and Jerusalem of idolatry (2 Chronicles 34:1-4). Elihu, son of Barakel the Buzite, said, "I am young in years and you are old; that is why I was fearful..." to speak (Job 32:6). He continued, "...it is the spirit in men, the breath of the Almighty, that gives him understanding. It is not only the old who are wise, not only the aged who understand what is right" (Job 32:8-9).

This spirit in man of which Elihu speaks, is that divine spark in us all that keeps us ever in attunement with God's Supreme Mind, Intelligence, and Consciousness. It is the only perfect essence in humans. It is indeed the "heaven within" of which Jesus Christ speaks, when asked in Mathews where heaven is as he explained that no one but the Father knows the "end of time." This spirit in us makes us true sons and daughters of God. It unites us—regardless of race, creed, economic status or education. It enables us to have equal access to God's universal and infallible intelligence. In other words, "if I can, so can you." Our limitations are only materialistic, objective, and psychological. After all, did not the bible say, "I can do all things through Christ who gives me strength" (Phil. 4:13). When empowered by Christ, our positions in life can change.

Job's three old friends gave him a real tongue lashing along with their perceptual reasoning why he, Job, was suffering the way he did. They all were wrong (Job 3:31). As the Bible says, "Age should speak: advanced years should teach wisdom" (Job 32:7). The emphasis is on the word 'should'. But this is not always the case— as we are all well aware. There are so many elders who act unwisely. If men do not fear the Lord, their wisdom is their personal conception, which is fallible.

The scriptures exhort, "Do not deceive yourselves. If any one of you thinks he is wise by the standards of this age, he should become a 'fool' so that he may become wise. For the wisdom of this world is foolishness in God's sight" (1 Corinthians 3:18-19). Here is where our minds play tricks on us; where pride hinders our progress, and where our human achievements deceive us as we feel that we know. Our ever changing human rights laws are reflections of our human folly as well as it boosts our efforts to continually improve to try to reflect the mind of God. What stunts our growth, what abbreviates our humanity is our presumption of knowledge—and our feeling that this human font of knowledge in the time we articulate it, is complete.

We must therefore seek an interpretation of realities and establish values through communion with the divine consciousness and intelligence of God. This is what Solomon did when he asked God for the ability to discern right from wrong and to have the understanding to administrate justly (1 Kings 3:9). Solomon here demonstrates humility and an acknowledgement that there is a power and intelligence superior to his.

The second error we make is in our manner of judging our personal development and growth. Since all our worldly achievements are meaningless as Solomon says (Ecclesiastes 2:17-26) and our main duty is to obey God's commands (Ecclesiastes 12:13); then our growth is determined by the measure of our obedience to Him and by the sincerity of our attunement with His Holy Spirit. Surely Solomon did not mean that to seek worldly achievements is unwise. He was obviously emphasizing the great value and importance of compliance with the directives of God. He later said we should enjoy life fully with our families (Ecclesiastes 9:9)

For God has said that He is the same, dependable God since the beginning (Malachi 3:6). He further said to test Him regarding His promises by obeying His commands and He will "...throw open the floodgates of heaven and pour out...much blessings" (Malachi 3:10). Clearly, the yardstick to use in measuring and determining where we are, consist of God's universal laws and principles.

It would indeed be impractical to ignore the standards and means of measurement in this world in which we live. Note that even Jesus Christ admonished the disciples that they ought to give Caesar what is Caesar's and to God what is God's (Matt. 22:21). Here is divine acknowledgement of the principle of respecting our value judgements of the world. For although they are fallible, they are what we have to work with now—today. No one can claim to be able to reflect the truth of absolute reality. No one's perception is perfect. But we all do possess that divine spark of God in us as says Elihu. Because of this, we have access to divine intelligence, and thus are each capable of bettering our positions in life and achieving more.

God did not literally place us where we are today—whether we are rich or poor, happy or sad, successful or unsuccessful. It is by our own choice that we are where we are. I will not digress into the argument of predestination versus free will. However, within both these philosophies discussing humanity's fate, there is clear evidence of agreement that humans do have, to some measure, the power to choose. Therefore, we each own some accountability for the level of achievements in our lives. It is this degree of accountability with which I am concern.

In reviewing the Cain and Abel's story, both had the desire to make offerings to God which they did. But Abel's was accepted, whilst Cain's was not. The Bible did not say or imply that God preferred Abel as a person to Cain, for God said to Cain, "Why are you so angry? Why is your face so downcast? If you do what is right, will you not be accepted" (Genesis 4:6-7)? The last question implies that God knew that Cain was aware of what he had to do; but he chose to do otherwise. Cain obviously had an equal chance for acceptance as did Abel. Even at this point, after finding out that his offering was "wrong" and that he did not find favour with God, he could have asked for forgiveness. Moreover, he could have asked his brother for a first born of the flock and do the "right" thing afterwards. Instead, Cain chose to nurture his anger and jealousy, thus giving evil more than a foothold (Ephesians 4:26-27). As a result, he deceived his trusting brother Abel by calling him into the fields and murdering him (Genesis 4:8).

The Bible says that righteous acts are done by the children of God; while unrighteous, by the children of the devil (1 John 3:9-10). This does not mean that Cain was a child of the devil, rather that Cain submitted to the devil's evil temptations. Surely the devil did not create anything or anyone. We know from biblical accounts that Cain was Abel's brother and the first born of Adam and Eve. Thus the Bible does not clearly mean that Cain was literally the devil's child; but that his action of obedience to the devil (his unrighteous behaviour) puts him in a paternal type relationship with the devil. Just as we are called sons and daughters of God because of our obedience to his wills and wishes, those performing unrighteous acts and thus are obedient to the wiles of the devil are called, biblically the children of the devil.

God is always pleased with our righteous behaviour. He blesses us with good health, prosperity, and a peaceful life. For He has said, "But seek first His kingdom and His righteousness, and all these things will be given to you as well" (Matthew 6:33). If we choose righteousness, we will be numbered among those who will always enjoy the abundance of life. We will be able to back our desires with knowledge and action and become true wishers and creators. Dr. Abraham H. Maslow referred to us as self-actualizing people. He said that, "Self-actualizing people enjoy life in general and in practically all its aspects, while most other people enjoy only strong moments of triumph, of achievement, of climax or of peak experience."

Needless to say, unrighteousness leads to disillusion, disappointment, and spiritual unfulfillment. Though Saul was the first king of God's chosen people, his unrighteous acts put him out of attunement and in disharmony with God's Holy Spirit. He was frequently tormented by his conscience such that only David's playing of inspiring and spiritually uplifting songs with the harp could soothe Saul momentarily. The Bible said that the Holy Spirit departed from Saul and that God sent an evil spirit to torment him (1 Samuel 16:14).

It is useful to digress a moment here and notice the challenging biblical statement that, '*God sent an evil spirit to torment Saul*' and that '*the Holy Spirit departed from Saul*'. From the premise that the Bible is God's Word and that within it, we know that God is a Holy God and says, "Be holy, for I am holy" (1 Peter 1:116; Leviticus 11:44-45), it is contradictory for him to be 'sending out evil spirits'— let alone possessing them. It seems to me at first, that the idea of God sending out an evil spirit is a ridiculous and illogical one. For Satan, the archenemy of God is the author of evil. Therefore, if an evil spirit would be sent to Saul, it would make more sense to come from Satan. But he would not torment Saul, for Saul was now obeying him and performing unrighteous acts. Any tormenting of Saul would thus constitute the inner conflicts and disharmony he experienced in his heart and conscience.

Saul knew right from wrong and he was well aware of his wrong choices. He was no longer hearing from God so he sought the advice from a witch (1 Samuel 28:7-14). But we can dispense with heavy semantics and hermeneutics in examining Saul's experiences. Let us put aside scholarly and academic exegetical methods. Saul's evil acts brought him much restlessness, guilt, and a search for inner peace. Clearly, God did not literally need to send an evil spirit to torment Saul, but it was his own conscience in the stillness of the nights pricking him and showing him how much he had moved away from the embrace and favour of God. It was the doubt he faced of the future and the fear of the end his kingship which his sons will not inherit. He no longer had divine guidance nor favour. Things were not going good and his enemies were almost upon him. He knew of the power and 'wrath' of God. He knew the consequences of his disloyalty, unfaithfulness, and the fate of all those who part company with God laws. His burdens were heavy and unbearable: thus his torment so great and tumultuous to seem like a spirit was upon him.

God did not forsake Saul. He cannot literally and logically forsake anyone. The Holy Spirit, who also is God, is immortal and omnipresent. How is it logically possible for an omnipresent being to depart any location or person on the universe of which that being has imbued? Can the water that is absorbed in a sponge, miss a specific spot, and yet soaks all the surrounding areas of that spot on the sponge? The Holy Spirit of God is immanent and transcendent. We know that Saul was so evil in his actions, which his mind and consciousness were clouded with such perfidious and unrighteous thoughts, that righteous and heavenly directives were now out of harmony with the new nature of his being.

Think of the sky. We all can and do have access to enjoy the stars and moon at nights and the direct radiations from the sun enjoining the bright blue daylight canopy of the heavens. But when the dust particles and dirt thickens and form the clouds, we lose sight of the heavenly beauty and can no longer witness the symphony of the spheres through our telescopes. The skies never and cannot go away, it is only the thick clouds that steps in which prevents us from seeing the stars at night. So it was with the Holy Spirit and Saul. The Spirit cannot go away. It was Saul's persistence to do evil, that stepped in and blocked the sweet and holy whispers from the Spirit of God.

If we do not want to end like Saul and instead have the better life: the life of inner peace and leisure, we must morally, by biblical standards, exercise our own volition and will. We neither obtain the good life by chance nor contingence. Nor will it simply appear to us upon one bright and sunny day—not even by trial and error. It will come to us without prejudice, race, creed, nationality or status; and by our personal and individual ambition, drive, and will to sacrifice our whims and fancies for the more worthy values. For the Holy Bible tells us that when we seek our Lord's righteousness, all other things will be given as well (Matthew 6:33).

We have to take the time to explore our true inner qualities and spiritual gifts; so that we have a better understanding of who we really are and why we feel and do the things we do. For instance, take the question of fate: does it control us? Or purpose: why are we here? We might say that these are philosophical and mystical questions. Perhaps, we would be wiser if we take a look at whether or not we are living a blueprint life: one that is mapped out for us by social and family pressures—or even by successful people. If so, where and what are the benefits we might receive. But even with these questions we cannot arrive at the correct answer to the know-how of experiencing the life of true peace and leisure; as our answer is dependent upon our unreliable perceptions and appraisals.

It is more beneficial to re-discover those creative forces within ourselves. They are our natural talents, education, skills, and abilities along with our spiritual gifts. These are creative forces like the bright stars that shine from the heavens at night, complementing the moon, our soul, to radiate the soft brilliance, our inner talents and knowledge that would guide us to achieve wealth, success, and happiness. So it is best we become experts at releasing such suppressed knowledge and inner abilities.

As we search ourselves, there is no reason why we should be embarrassed when we realize that the idea we thought to be a brilliant one has failed. The thoroughfare of life has sufficient evidence to verify that the experience of an occasional failure is inevitable when one is going after success in his or her personal affairs, business undertakings, or spiritual aspirations. One Chinese philosopher observed that success is the lurking place of failure. Of course, this does not mean that we must have a sense of accomplishment when we fail; rather, we must not permit ourselves to be sucked into the black hole of discouragement. We must remember the maxim, 'We learn by our experiences—good or bad'. And the Bible says, "Happy (blessed, fortunate, enviable) is the [person] who finds skilful and godly Wisdom, and the [person] who gets understanding [drawing it forth from God's Word and life's experiences]..." (Pro. 3:13, *Amplified Bible*)

James Allen said, in his book, "As A Man Thinketh," "Every man is where he is by the law of his being; the thoughts which he has built into his character have brought him there, and in the arrangement of his life there is no element of chance, but all is the result of a law which cannot err. This is just as true of those who feel 'out of harmony' with their surroundings as of those who are contented with them." Thus we are our thoughts. These energised principles plague us behind the scenes and cause us to be who we are and do the things we do and feel.

For example, the gap in the earnings between the rich and the poor, in the performance between the amateur and the expert, is not a result of fate or fortune; but thought and law. When our earnings are not up to our expectations, and our level of development is not to the point we desire, we are responsible. We obviously lack know-how, self motivation, and optimism. Self-doubt most times holds us back. We would read of the accomplishments of successful persons, and in our minds we would echo, "They have done it again." Then in wishful thinking we whisper, "I wish some of their luck would rub off on me." We would not, instead of this, add action to our thoughts and bring our wishes and hopes to materialization. For the Bible says, "Faith by itself, if it is not accompanied with action, is dead" (James 2:17). Here the bible separates the pure dreamers from the doers. The bible does not put down the dreamers, however; for Christ told us that whatever we want or desire, we must just believe that we have it and pray and ask for it in his name and we will get it (Mark 11:24). This lesson helps us to understand, that Jesus Christ as God, is able and we can rely on Him. When we prayer by faith, God will draw us to the circumstances and condition wherein and whereby our faithful prayers will be answered.

But there comes a time when we can begin to act—just as we

have read or heard the success stories of others. It is here and now we should be motivated by their attainments, and begin thinking of how to emulate them. This is the moment our aspirations should be stimulated; our dreams, more clearly visualized; and our courage stirred to an explosive pitch where we should be motivated to act immediately.

Since no one but ourself is in charge of our financial position and development level, it is our responsibility alone to search out better ways towards opulence and to commune with the consciousness of Christ. For the Bible says that the measure we give will determine our receipts (Matthew 7:2). We can become wealthy: materially and spiritually. The Bible says that when we seek God's kingdom and His righteousness, we will have eternal life and "all other" blessings "as well." The big question is whether we are prepared to make the necessary sacrifices and to be persistent in our efforts.

Many of us, when we encounter difficulties, back down in a corner crying out for help from someone else, instead of making some real effort to help ourselves. And if we fail, we become disappointed and defeated, losing vigour and vitality which we had when we began. The truth is, we cannot erase nor will away the memory of our failures, but as we are alive now, we can do something to effect a better future. The idea is not to sit in hope that God will come down from heaven and solve our problems for us; but that we should make the first move now—today. The good news is God wants us all to be rich and wealthy. He wants to give us exceedingly and in abundance (Eph. 3:20)

Often the problem is our state of mind. Of course, if we would hold envious, spiteful, and negative thoughts in our minds, our face cannot portray warmth and friendliness. Even if it did, people would feel it; that is, sense it. Furthermore, our eyes would have such an evil look, that it would be clear enough for almost anyone to discern our true emotions. For I have heard the 'old folks' say that the eyes are the windows of or doorway to the soul. Jesus said, "Your eye is the lamp of your body. When your eyes are good, your whole body is full of light. But when they are bad, your body also is full of darkness" (Luke 11:34).

We must therefore replace our vanity with modesty and remove fear and pessimism by filling our mind with positive and constructive thoughts. We must smile a sincere smile as we look forward to a successful day and many happy tomorrows. If we do this, it means we are coping with the laws of life. Success and happiness will then be inevitable; victory, a slave under our command. We become true architects and construction engineers of our personal lives, ambitions, and goals.

There can be no victory, however, without a plan; no materialization without design; no summits without graduated levels. Impulsive decisions and actions mean sure failures. Not even God acted without a plan: He thought, decided, and then visualized the world before creating it. We, therefore, are subject to these same universal principles and regulations, and where we are today is determined by how we apply these laws.

The Value of an Experience

I remember those times of joy, of optimism, and of drive. I remember those wonderful moments of gaiety, those abstruse meanings of life, those irrevocable urges to succeed and fulfil some unselfish goal I set myself. To me, then, there were beauty and purpose in my life. But of those times I yielded to temptations and clutched to the easy way out, I experienced the depth of sadness and the tortures and the ugliness that compliment indolence, sin, and negative thinking.

In reflection I wondered about life's experiences. What are they really? How do they come into existence? Are they out there, somewhere awaiting us—set out in a kind of maze? Maybe if we take one path, a specific group of experiences we are bound to encounter; and if we were to take another, there is another group of experiences for us to meet. Can we escape experiences, control them, and master them as if they were games? Do we set them off—somehow creating them? Or are they assigned to us by some divine, fatalistic scheme?

Most certainly, these are very interesting questions. Their answers, if they exist, would undoubtedly give us great ease, and perhaps enormously remove the stresses and worries from our lives. But this will run counter to God's edict that there will always be active enmity between humankind and "the evil forces" (Genesis 3:5). There is no perfect peace until the *end of time*. Although, a life with packaged answers to the above questions may indeed make our journey from birth to transition less burdensome. It would be an added "blessing" if we did not have to be disturbed with such matters like experiences—at least the painful ones. Most of us do not like the uncertainty of their outcomes with their associated pain. As normal humans we have extended tolerance for pleasurable experiences.

But is this simply foolish musings: that is, to consider a life without any kind of experience? Immediately something in me shudders with this kind of thinking; for life and experience are not mutually exclusive. We cannot have one without the other. Life is being. Being is. It exists. It implies the quality of awareness or consciousness. It is therefore sensitive—this requires stimuli and responses, actions and reactions. With life or the having of it we can at least know things. Solomon said, "...the living know that they would die, but the dead know nothing" (Ecclesiastes 9:5). David said to God in prayer, "No one remembers you when he is dead. Who praises you from the grave" (Psalm 6:5). Life comprises activities, events, doing, and feeling.

We can indeed praise God when we are alive. As Solomon said of the dead, "Their love, their hate and their jealousy have long since vanished; never again will they have a part in anything that happens under the sun" (Ecclesiastes 11:6). Solomon is speaking strictly about life on earth. After the Resurrection, we will have life again—forever. In the same chapter of the Bible, he said that we should enjoy our lives as much as possible; for in death, there is no working, nor planning nor knowledge nor wisdom. He advises us that whatever we find to do, do it mightily. We therefore must not leave it for tomorrow, as says an ancient manuscript of wisdom.

We have indicated here why we must be involved in activities while we are alive. Non-activity is similar to death. After all, Solomon said, "Go, eat your food with gladness,...always be clothed with white" (Ecclesiastes 7:9). We cannot continue to exist without food; maybe we could remain in some place like the garden of Eden in the nude, provided that there was an endless supply of food as fruits and vegetables. But now we are becoming ridiculous and we must hasten back to the realities of life as we know it.

With the coming of the developers, the population explosion, there are not many Eden-like places to live. Let us not conclude that nudist beaches are like the Garden of Eden. We all have to work to eat, clothe, and shelter ourselves as well as to ensure the continuity of the human race. No one can escape this pronouncement (Genesis 3:16.17,19).

My friend Michelle, while we walked said to me, "Life is hard and life is sweet," as she contemplated the joys and sorrows of her yesterdays. Tears began to form in her eyes. But in an effort to withhold them, she tried to smile turning her face away from me. But her tears took no heed: they flowed undisturbed and without consideration, despite her earnest attempt to conceal them. "Please, please don't come to my eyes," I imagined she pleaded.

A tremor—a kind of heartache—struck me. I began thinking: Why the hardships—then moments of happiness. Why the failures?—then the heartfelt successes. This all seem inevitable—the duality of the positive and the negative. We can neither deny nor accept one without the other.

This duality of life experience can be placed in one of two groups by identifying which of our feelings are painful or pleasurable. For the sake of argument, painful experiences hurt and pleasurable ones feel good or do not hurt at all. When we are calm, at peace, or at rest, such a tranquil state is without discomfort and therefore it is pleasurable.

Still, what can we truly say is an experience? We know we have them or rather, we are involved in them. This knowing is a kind of awareness we have of our experiences. Although we observe someone else's experience: hear or see or read it, these are all conscious occurrences. We speak of an experience here as though it is somehow outside ourselves, something separate. As if it has an existence independent of us—like an object. To quickly remove this view, we do not normally point and say, for example, "there is an experience," or "Can you not see it down there" while looking at it as something spatial; that is, having a distinct position in time and space. We always think of experience in a personal way, having a reality only in relation to ourselves or someone else.

In life, we see that an experience may consist of one or more incidents. It may either be deliberate or accidental. It is not a condition of fate nor fortune, but an aftermath, bounded by unchangeable laws which we set off by our thoughts and deeds. Somehow, sometime, somewhere, we have thought, said, or done something to experience the joys, the sorrows, and the marvels of life. Although God assigned us a specific experience as a test or trial from which we are to learn and grow in a divinely planned way, it is we alone, no matter how absurd this may seem, who are responsible for our accidents, luck, and even mysterious coincidences. Perhaps it may be Satan who placed it in our paths as a stumbling block, and it is still up to us to learn from it. After all, we could have chosen not to be at the place of the experience, or we could have chosen not to fear the Lord and be qualified like Job for any measure of tests and trials. We could have chosen not to do anything in a particular circumstance and simply float along and so be a victim or victor then saying we are either unlucky or lucky. Our very inaction here is in fact an action—it is causal, it is a specific option we have taken or chosen.

Often, we are so absorbed with the unpleasantness of our experiences, that we fail to spot their possible causes. We delay upon those mental conditions instead of taking immediate steps to attend to them. This delay costs us our greatest embarrassments and hardships—and sometimes, even our sanity. For as we dwell upon those transient sorrows, the seeds, from which they blossom, spring roots that seep deeper into the centres of our hearts and minds. Thus, after a short period, we form mountains out of molehills.

It is only when our experiences become excruciating and unbearable, do we begin to take steps to pacify them. If our efforts have been frustrated by time and wrong diagnoses, we cry out dishearteningly for help. We soon remember the existence of God, whom we had forgotten for quite sometime. We began to pray, to attend church regularly, and to study the Bible. As usual, it took ordeals for us to be cognizant with His omniscience and our duty to worship Him, to thank Him, and to praise Him.

But He had no direct dealings with our hardships; though He at times tests us. It is we, by our choice and will, who wrap the ropes of sadness about ourselves, blaming the devil and thereafter asking God for deliverance. When we violate His laws and regulations by our disobedience, we must be prepared to accept responsibility. This is the indirect way in which our Lord is involved in the hardships we bring upon ourselves. But the devil tempts us too—making us digress from the righteous path of life.

Ethan, the Levite, wrote God's response to Israel's continual disobedience to Him: "If his sons forsake my law and do not follow my statues, if they violate my decrees and fail to keep my commands, I will punish their sin with the rod, their iniquity with flogging" (Psalm 89:30-32). Now we must pay very special attention to the fairness and impartiality of our God. He was punishing Israel's 'sin' and 'iniquity'. Note that He said, "I will punish their sin" and "their iniquity.

Further, He made it clear when He said, "but I will not take my love from him, nor will I betray my faithfulness. I will not violate my covenant or alter what my lips have uttered" (Psalm 89:33,34). It is important for us to realize that God punishes the sin and not the sinner, the crime and not the criminal, the wrong deed and not the doer. He still maintains His love for us, in spite of what we do. So too, must we behave in our relationships: deal with the problem and not be angry with or condemn our friends, brothers and sisters, and spouses. We must hate racism and not the racist, homosexuality and not the homosexual or gay person.

On the other hand, we have said that God sometimes tests us and Satan always temps us. This is true. We see how confident God was about the ability of His servant Job. So He felt that Job, by his own choice to persistently fear the Lord and cooperate with the divine laws, had a developed (or an awakened) soul personality that was indeed worthy and ready to undergo the trials of the 'dark night'. In the end, Job was greatly rewarded as he showed his loyalty to the Lord and because during the time when "the shadows," the doubts and troubles came upon him, he sought to commune with God for deliverance. In 1 Peter 1:1-11, the apostle Peter spoke of the grief, the suffering, the trials God puts us through to test our faith, refine our character. He said that in the end, when we endure, we receive the goal of our faith, the salvation of our souls.

During difficulties, either caused by our disobedience or our worthiness, we do not have to yield to the temptations of the devil. We can choose not to do so. But perhaps it is the nature of man to comply with the desires of his 'old self'. The Bible says, "The man without the Spirit does not accept things that come from the Spirit of God, for they are foolishness to him, and he cannot understand them, because they are spiritually discerned" (1 Corinthians 2:14). We have to regenerate ourselves, by yielding to the Christhood of Jesus; by hiding ourselves with Him in God (Colossians 3:3).

Yet with all the harsh realities of life, we cannot deny the benefits we derive. We cannot hide, far more obliterate from our minds, the good that comes into our lives along with life's hardships. That our experiences may often times be painful, is fact. But, that with these pains we gain some object of knowledge, is fact too. We must be contented with this knowledge, rather than brood over yesterday's difficulties.

It is all well and good to pray that we are spared life's burdens— like somebody beside ourselves places them upon our shoulders saying, "this cross is yours and yours alone to bear"; but it is quite another matter to pray for knowledge, wisdom, and guidance toward success and the good life. If we are honest, we will realize that each time we try to escape from our problems, it is we who have created them ourselves: not God nor the devil. It is by our will we choose righteous or unrighteous behaviour.

Both Eve and Adam could have chosen to disregard Satan. They knew that God Almighty was supreme, for after they submitted to the wiles of the devil and disobeyed God (Genesis 3:6,7), they felt guilty and their conscience tormented them (Genesis 3:10). That is why they 'hid' from God when He was 'calling' them in the Garden. Though their conscience was troubling them, they tried to justify their behaviour; for both Eve and Adam, passed the buck' on to their vile natures, to the dragons and devils that plague the hearts of men (Genesis 3:12,13).

St. Paul said, "Each one should test his own actions. Then he can take pride in himself, without comparing himself to somebody else, for each one should carry his own load" (Galatians 6:4,5). With this in mind therefore, we should find it easier to master our lives knowing that it is primarily up to us. The divine laws and the Holy Spirit are accessible to all. No longer are we to pay for our parents' sins.

The experience of pain and pleasure lies in our hands; and we should exercise a greater watchfulness over what we think, say, or do. Since, as John Locke, an English philosopher, said, that "No man's knowledge here can go beyond his experience." And of knowledge, Shakespeare said it is "…the wing wherewith we fly to heaven…." Then the value of an experience is not so much the knowledge we gain from it, but how much of it we put to constructive use and by how much did it help us to attain the 'good life'.

Personal Magnetism

The Bible does not concur with astrology as a means for us to determine our life's goals and for us to understand who we are in Christ. As Bible believing Christians, we would feel guilty if we would seek to know God's will in our lives through astrology. In fact, the Bible warns us against the use of stargazers and astrologers (Isa. 47:13-14). In our human relationships, we at best, will live fully and agreeably if we seek to adopt Christlike attitudes (1 Cor. 4:15-16, NKJV). The pattern of the stars cannot tell us how to live and treat others. We are followers of our Lord Jesus Christ who was God incarnate while he lived on earth. We will therefore attract everyone who are of God and repel those who are not. Thus those who seek to be God fearing, will naturally be likeminded and be attracted to each other. These imitators of Christ will undoubtedly repel attitudes and methods that dishonour God—those attitudes that violate his rules and purposes.

Still, we observe the Bible has recorded the "sharp disagreement" between Paul and Barnabas (Acts 15:39). They could not work together, despite their unquestionable devotion to the gospel of Jesus Christ, the great commission, and their obvious love for the things of God. The position of the moon, stars, and planets were not responsible for their disagreement. Their personal views and perceptions were (Acts 15:37-38). It is our thoughts and views which make us who we are. The Bible says, "as a man thinks in his heart, so is he" (Prov.

23:7). Paul and Barnabas both continued to serve the Lord, but had to go separate ways (Acts 15:39-40). Even in our modern times, there are contentious issues arising out of the different and divergent interpretations of the Scriptures. Within the evangelical spectrum of beliefs, the existence of Pentecostals, Baptists, Protestants, and so on informs us that some evangelicals are attracted to one view and others, another. The reality of attraction and repulsion exist concurrently with our belief in salvation through Jesus Christ, the great commission, and in Jesus' second coming.

Attraction and repulsion are the key characteristics of magnetism. These happen between two or more entities or bodies. Usually we note these characteristics in material substances; but modern day human relationship experts use them as well when describing the relationships between people. This usage, however, is not new at all, as the ancients have long observed the polemic qualities in human personalities and in fact, in all existences. A cursory examination of ancient studies of mysticism and even astrology would testify to this truth.

Causality, the study of cause and effect, as a universal principle is premised on the doctrine of polarity. Many philosophers, ancient and modern, have addressed this topic. For example, Aristotle wrote that there are four causes and Hume concluded that there are two definitions for causation. According to modern mystical philosophers, causality is related to the study of magnetism as well since in magnetism there is a stage prior to the magnets being in contact with each other. This antecedent stage is where the cause lies. The proceeding stage, the results of the interaction of the magnetic forces, is the effect.

Popular opinion holds that for every cause, there is an effect. This generally means that both the cause and the effect are singular in nature. However, some modern mystics observed that there are other laws underlying the occurrence or the reality of the effect. Here the study of polarity is significant. Since, as claimed, the cause produces the effect which is real, then there must of necessity involve two polemically opposite qualities—a passive and an active—

combining together as one cause to result in the known effect.

Assuming all of the above to be true, what does it have to do with personal magnetism—that is, with you and I meeting each other and either liking or disliking one another's company? What role, if any, does our conscience play in all of this? We know that in the ancient studies of astrology, polarity and causality play important roles in human relationships.

In the study of polarity, we know that persons with complimenting qualities make the best team members. Thus stated, we may construe complimentary qualities as polemic opposites. We are not talking about two persons who hate each other, nor are we talking about individuals with necessarily opposing views. Certainly such persons could not work well on the same team—there would be needless dissipation of energies in contentions and conflicts. Rather, polemic personalities refer to persons, despite their differences in views or opinions, can arrive at a point wherein they can set aside these differences as they have overlapping views on more important issues.

With reference to causality, we can best understand the resultant state of relationships. In other words, if the relationship is agreeable or disagreeable, this determination is the effect. The cause would be the active polemic blending of the personalities involved. Therefore, if the spirits of the participants are congenial, we find an effectual agreeableness; otherwise, the converse results.

Our conscience provides a stabilizing role. Depending on its state, our conscience keeps us in check and can be the key in maintaining and sustaining the good health of our relationships. With a weak conscience, we will shift in our values and so be inconsistent and unreliable. This leads to disappointment and frustrations. Later, antagonisms and dissentions set in. With a strong (or theonomous) conscience, we keep the relationship consistent, stable, and governed by God's will and purposes. Even when there are disagreements, our strong conscience emphasizes our morality and pliability. Paul says, "I speak the truth in Christ—I am not lying, my conscience confirms it in the Holy Spirit..." (Rom. 9:1). Here we have no regrets, as our strong conscience assures us that our actions are in accord to God's will. If all participants can emulate Paul, then in relationships, we would be able to disagree and still be agreeable.

This is exactly what Paul and Barnabas did. Despite their 'sharp disagreement', they parted and continued to do God's work. We can be certain there was no hate between them. For such would run counter to the very gospel message they so enthusiastically delivered. Even in relationships where there may be un-Christlike views and values, God can use such relationships to fulfil His purposes. God because of who He is can cross the boundaries and intervene or interrupt cosmic laws. When from a human standpoint we may deem a relationship impossible, God can do the unthinkable and make it work to fulfil his purposes. For instance, God instructed the prophet Hosea to marry the prostitute Gomer (Hosea 1:1-2); God allowed the Israelite Boaz to marry the pagan Moabitist Ruth (Ruth 4:13); Joseph, who saved the Israelites from starvation was given an Egyptian wife Asenath (Gen. 41:45); and the pagan King Ahasuerus made Esther, the daughter of Mordecai the Jew, his queen (Esther 2:17).

These incredible relationships succeeded and we may point out that God's purposes were fulfilled. These relationships were outside the principles of the positive outcomes of personal magnetism and were contrary to the very rules and laws that make relationships congenial and lasting. But God established each in accordance to His will. There was no compliance with any rules of astrology, numerology, palmistry, phrenology, or any of the occult arts or psychic methodologies. God is able to do whatever he chooses. He has always been a God of impossibilities. Moses witnessed burning bush that was not consumed by the fire (Ex. 3:3); Moses caused the red sea to part so that the Israelites could safely walk across to the other side (Ex. 14:15-31); Daniel remained alive in a hungry lions den (Dan. 6:20-22); Mary and Joseph had angels appear to them (Lk. 1:26; Matt. 2:13; 28:2); angels appeared to the shepherds to inform them of the birth of the Christ (Lk. 2:9-10); three magis or stargazers knew of Jesus' birth and location (matt. 2:1-2; 2:9-11); Apostle Peter was freed from prison by an angel (Acts 5:19); the Apostle Paul and

Silas' prayers literally shook the prison, "…all the doors were flung opened, and everyone's chains were loosed" (Acts 16:25-26).

It is this same wonder working God who created the universe and all within it. All things and existences do have a common thread and must necessarily be related. When we are born, there must have been a relationship between ourselves and the existences around us—the stars, the moon, the plants, the animals, the sun and all other living and nonliving things. Particle physicists prove that all existences are vibratory. Just as water—being vibratory—when heated in a kettle or test tube boils as the heat energy excites the test tube or the kettle and in turn the water particles or molecules are excited and affected—becoming hot. So does every existence affect another with which it is in contact. This is the interconnectivity of the Law at work. Here is a demonstration of its universality. We may doubt it, but we run against commonsense and the very logic of the nature of our being in relationships. Our denial does not nullify the effect we have on others or the effect that they have on us by one iota.

We know for a fact that we like or dislike people—even when we may only just have met them. We say often that we are attracted to this person and, another may be repulsed by us. We talk of getting "negative or positive vibes" from friends or potential customers or business partners and even family. This polemic language we use in how we relate to others is a reflection of how we relate magnetically. This language forms the basis for our present examination of the experience we call *personal magnetism.*

It is customary in our societies—in the newspapers, magazines, TV programs, and websites—to be told that planetary bodies do have an influence on our personalities. Research has shown that sun spots, the moon, the presence of groups of ions in our atmosphere affect many conditions on earth. But as to the controlling of our urges and tendencies is another matter. They may influence us just as Satan may tempt us or God may speak to us. But they do not compel us to act. We blame alcoholism and drug addiction for the incumbent's unruly behaviour. We blame the substance, not the user. But the substances possess no will and cannot act on their own. Yet their presence in the physical body affect the brain and so the perceptions of the user. In this way such substances influence a person's behaviour. Many substances and existences may influence and cause us to act in one way or another. But in the end, we are accountable.

We know that the moon affects the waters on earth. We are taught in grade 12 that 98% of our physical bodies consist of liquid. We can safely assume, as laypersons, that the moon should have some effect on us. It is no wonder that the unusual reactions of mentally ill persons along with the moon changes gave rise to their being called "lunatics." In the so-called new field of biorhythms, we learn about the effects of cosmic bodies, sun rays, and lunar influences on life on earth. We are increasingly arriving at more scientific data that is giving some credence to the fundamental truths of ancient astrology. Psychology has often set aside these as false or as practices that are primarily founded on superstition. Yet parapsychology has been incorporating the fundamentals of old truisms in its body of knowledge. Still, these validations do not justify our dependence on astrology for guidance on living Christlike lives.

That persons born "under the same zodiac signs" do possess similar tendencies, may at times be true. However, I am neither an astrologer nor cosmologist to authoritatively make such a claim. But as a Christians we must know that "similar tendencies" is an undependable phrase. Astrologers cannot and do not claim their readings are precise or perfect—even though the language of their readings are very persuasive and positive. For this reason, we ought to remember the Biblical admonition to avoid dependence on stargazers or astrologers (Isa. 47:13-14; Dan. 5:15).

It would be unwise for anyone to determine their life goals based on a set of unreliable data. Biblically speaking, Christians know that "All Scripture is given by inspiration of God…that the man [person] of God may be complete, thoroughly equipped for every good work" (2 Tim. 3:16-17). Further, we know that, "Every word of God is pure [flawless]…" (Prov. 30:5-6). Added to these, God knows us from the womb of our mothers—before we are born (Gen. 25:23; Jer. 1:5). For God's knowledge is perfect (Job. 36:4). Finally, we, by prayer and faith, can "…be filled with the knowledge of [God's] will in all wisdom and spiritual understanding; that [we] may walk worthy of the Lord, fully pleasing Him, fruitful in every good work and increasing in the knowledge of God" (Col. 1:9).

Realistically speaking, several persons may be affected by a similar vibratory arrangement from a specific group of planetary bodies. This depends on their time and place of birth. But astrological readings are not in sync with God's will for our lives. People differ because of free will, unique life experiences, hereditary, God purposes, and spiritual development. Again, we emphasize dependence on God's word and not astrology or any of the occult arts.

Another subject of intrigue, concerns the condition of two personalities naturally clashing or blending. This has led us to a pet suggestion of soul mates. The puzzling contradiction to the soul mates idea is when two people fall deeply in love, have a wonderful relationship and after many years, break up. Many 'soul mates' supporters later defensively contend that the persons were mismatched. Several differences in their qualities are then shown to prove that there was obviously a mismatching of qualities and thus the reasons for the inevitable breakdown in the relationship. The obvious perception here is that soul mates would be forever together—for they were meant to be.

One may argue that soul mates are also individuals with the power to choose. They may choose not to comply with the necessary acts that allow them to fulfil their destined relationship. Soul mates are a product of the predestination philosophy. The scriptures as well as our life experiences are clear on this issue. From the beginning, both Adam and Eve—the first soul mates—chose to be disobedient. Now they did not separate—they just sinned together. Not being facetious, but they were true soul mates indeed. In the Genesis account, we know neither had a choice of a different mate since they were the only two humans. They obviously had a cooperative and congenial relationship as far as we can tell. God never intervened much or had to do much counselling from on high—except of course, for the one major issue disobedience wherein their both being accountable for creating problems for us in our relationship with God from our very birth. One thing we notice is that there were no compromises. Adam blamed God and Eve and Eve blamed the Serpent.

Later in the Bible, we see God's people tended to keep their marriage vows. Naturally there were many instances in separation, adultery, and prostitution. Often it was the mixture of God's people with other races and cultures that caused the sins and marriage breakdowns. The marriages by divine degree—or the support for soul mate doctrines—were normally successful. Now just as there were no compromises in the "*the fall contention*" involving Adam and Eve, even as God orchestrated and ordained the family blood line towards the parenthood of Jesus Christ, often along the path we see humans exercising their own will and reason that could have put the route offline. Notice that Sarah sent her servant Haggai to give Abraham a son; Isaac wanted to bless his first born Esau; Jacob was tricked by Laban to marry Leah and not Rachel; Joseph was sold into slavery by his brothers; and this continued to the Jewish King Herod wanting to kill Jesus at birth.

How do we juggle the ideas of the divine plan and free will in relationships? Jesus' mission was to save the world, but his path was filled with temptations designed to make him stray from God's plan. Satan began his temptations from Jesus' first days of fasting in the wilderness. This continued throughout Christ's ministry, and up to Jesus' time in the garden of Gethsemane. Jesus had the opportunity and power to disobey, to run counter to divine will and plan; but he chose not to. We can assume too that even when soul mates meet, there is no universal or divine law compelling them to stay together. As perfect a match as they may be, the persuasiveness of temptations and the pride that accompany free will, are always in conflict and contention with what God wants for his children.

Throughout our lives we make choices to meet our needs, desires, and goals. Although the Israelites were chosen by God, they have frequently opted to sin against Him. He punished them many times but still upon their repentance, He returned favours and blessings to them. Finally, Israel was divided: becoming Judah and Jerusalem. In a sense here is an example of a truly divine relationship: God and the Israelites, and it did not work out the way one would have expected it to as in any divine relationship.

Let us look further: Saul was anointed but look at his behaviour which led him to lose favour in the eyes of God. What then of Judas Iscariot? Was he destined by our loving, just and merciful God to be one of the greatest traitors ever known to man? Was he, as some think, an approbate soul? We all know that according to the Bible, he betrayed the trust of Jesus. Did Jesus know that Judas will betray Him at the point of making him a disciple but still went ahead, anyway, to accept him amongst His closest followers because of His mission? I find this hard to believe. But since God *knows the future*, He must have known what Judas would do. And as one twentieth century mystical philosopher would say, '*God knowing the tendencies and proclivities of an individual [like Judas], does not mean a compulsion of Judas' will and reason*'.

We must realize that Jesus did not know everything. He himself said to His disciples when they asked him about His second coming, that "No one knows about that day or hour, not even the angels in heaven, nor the Son, but only the Father" (Matthew 24:36). The Bible did not tell us that when He saw Judas, He knew Judas was the destined traitor and so He chose him. Judas's intentions were initially good. But later, Judas changed by his own choice and yielding to negative promptings and evil temptations.

If we disagree with this view, we must remember that Satan cannot create anything. Therefore, we must conclude that God created this evil soul called Judas, who was destined to 'sell Jesus for thirty pieces of silver'. But it is most difficult for us to believe in a God who is just, merciful, and loving and who, at the same time, would preordain evil to prove He is Almighty. We may say, "God is God and He does as He pleases"; but such vanity and conceit have no place in the heart and mind of the God of the Christian Bible. Why does He have to prove anything to us at all or to Himself? We need Him and not He needs us. He is our creator; we are His creatures.

We notice since time immemorial, that in almost any circumstance or condition, there are several alternatives: more than one solution, many options. The 'soul mates' philosophy runs contrary to this incontestable reality. If having soul mates were true, we would ultimately choose the mates destined for us. To do otherwise, is to make a mockery of the entire philosophy of predestination and of the power and sovereignty of God. For whatever God ordains is unchangeable law.

In prayer and in meditation individuals can be prompted by the Holy Spirit. In their inner consciousness they can be incited to take a specific course of action and not take another. They may experience a strong hunch to chose one person and not another or to simply wait. Since no one they know at the time possesses the harmonious qualities that will lead to a meaningful and lasting relation, we can understand the intervention of our perfect, impartial, and loving God. But remember, it is a prompting, not an order—not a compulsion.

Saul did not work out, though he was anointed and chosen. Let us remember that Saul never repented, never showed remorse. Naturally another more suitable person (David) was found to replace him. This kind of God makes much sense to us and truly measures up to fairness, mercy, and love. Later David sinned in committing adultery with Bathsheba. He also engineered the death of Bathsheba's Hitite husband. David then sincerely repented and paid the price by an impartial law of compensation. God took the life of the first child of David and Bathsheba. By another law of mercy, he was forgiven though he was not allowed the privilege of building the house for the Lord. His former action made him an unworthy and unsuitable builder. But one of his sons, Solomon, according to God's promise, was granted the honour. God punishes the sin and the iniquity not the sinner (Psalm 89:33) and He keeps His promises—He loved the man, the sinner David (Psalm 89:34). He loves us too, that is why He sacrificed His son's, Jesus', life to save the world (John. 3:16).

In dealing with people, we can always identify a specific trait they display that may turn us on or off. We may, for instance, be turned off by an overly aggressive behaviour or a boastful attitude. We may, on the other hand, be turned on by a meek or a helpful disposition. Yet another person may like the aggressiveness in others, it seems that in relationships, and including new ones, we attract or repel one another. We are not talking about human relations skills or about how-to-do-it techniques of getting along with people. Rather, we are making a preliminary observation of the forces at work that cause attraction and repulsion among people in relationships—or even for a first time interaction. We have called this examination, this subject of study, Personal Magnetism.

In physics, we learn of magnetic forces. We learn that like or similar poles of a magnet repel and that unlike poles attract. Repel is to push against or cause to move away from each other, while attract is to call towards.

In our high school study of magnetism, we learned that metals, because of their inner make-up, when put within the 'reach' of the magnetic lines of force or close to the magnet, themselves become magnets—having both north and south poles. These 'potential magnets' must either be within the area of influence called the magnetic field or actually in direct contact with a magnet to become magnetized. This behaviour, one must agree is indeed fascinating between substances. On the other hand, there are those substances, like wood, that are apparently not affected at all by the presence of a magnet. If they are affected, then the influence or effect is so infinitesimally small, that it is negligible.

The point here is for us to realize that it is the emanation of rays, about a magnetic substance, that projects to effect and influence a nearby object that is a potential magnet and thus affecting and changing the behaviour of the latter. I am not qualified to discuss the subject of magnetism in its entirety and in the multiplicity of ways in which it manifests itself. My knowledge of physics is limited. However, it is fascinating to notice a similarity in the magnetism between substances and the 'Personal Magnetism in human relationships'.

I am not saying that the magnetic principles are applied in the exact way in human relations as they do with substances. Rather, I am saying an examination of its operations in the latter would help us to better understand how it operates in the former. Note too that all these laws are not written and stated in the Holy Scriptures, though many scriptures have inspired scientific investigations. However, our life experiences and history of people in relationships testify to the presence of the magnetism among people. Our denial would not in any way change this eternal truth: that humans do attract and repel one another in relationships.

Students of physics, and we can too, learn that there are lines of forces that emanate and surround a magnet. Any basic science book with experiments with magnets would have the popular experiment with magnets and iron filings to show the magnetic lines of force. Now once another magnet or potential magnet is within the area of the lines of force (called the magnetic field) of the primary magnet, there is a resultant effect. The iron filings show the traces of the path of the uniting or repelling lines of force. For when two forces clash or interact, there is a reaction or change from the initial state.

In fact, research has shown with photography and electricity, that all living organisms do have about them a magnetic field. This magnetic field, in humans, many call the aura. Even if we are sceptical, we cannot argue with what we so often experience when we meet people we just feel an affinity to and others, whose personalities just antagonize us. Because we feel something desirable or undesirable means that our senses were actuated by some kind of invisible stimuli. After all, we, upon first meeting of a well dressed and well mannered person with whom we have not said anything to and vice versa, may simply have an instant dislike for them. We have in popular jargon 'picked up negative vibes,' despite the respectable and likeable appearance. I am not speaking of our evaluation of their personal appearance and whether or not we like their attire.

What causes this repulsion and sometimes attraction? What are the true principles involved? A relationship is a situation that exists only as a result of two or more persons having some kind of contact or involvement. Personal magnetism exists either when we just meet someone as well as when we have some level of interaction with the person. Marriages, families, and organizations are all examples of relationships in which we interact with people to some degree. John alone could not have a relationship; nor could Michelle. Yet one of them will have to begin the contact or involvement. Somebody has to make the first move. The prime mover is the active principle; the person against or towards whom the move was made is the passive.

One of the major challenges in human relationships is our ability to affect the relationships in a way we desire. In other words, how to make a person like us who presently does not? Or more daringly: why would a person who disliked us previously, now look at us favourably? This is the challenge for human relationship experts.

A change of mind or a change of feelings suggest that likes and dislikes are not static or permanent emotional states of being or self-expression. They depend upon the cooperation of the forces between ourselves and the people with whom we come into contact. That is, how we feel after our auras interact with another person's.

When we like a person, we find them pleasant; their personality traits harmonize with our values or standards. Since in the cases when we never communicated with such persons we have a resultant feeling; then our force fields or lines of force must in some way be in harmony with the person's. Like magnets, their inherent qualities are represented by their external lines of force or their aura which in turn blended with ours.

As stated earlier, these inner qualities are what we put into our hearts, our conscience by mundane and spiritual experiences. Once again we imply the power and life of words. To change our minds or feelings towards the person, would be to change our values or standards, or the person having to change theirs.

Thoughts exit. They must therefore be vibratory in nature since, as science has proven, all matter is made up of energy which is vibratory. The Bible tells us that Jesus 'knew' what the Pharisees were thinking when they were jealously criticizing his actions of telling the lame man that his sins were forgiven. Christ responded to them (Matthew 9:4-6) by saying that the Son man has authority on earth to forgive sins. Note that the Bible says Jesus 'knowing their thoughts...'.

Besides, very often many of us have had the experience of thinking of a song or idea and suddenly someone in our presence would begin to sing the same song or to express the same idea. This is too common an experience to call it co-incidence. We are reminded of a radio or television station that is a source of transmitting a program or news. Any radio or television set can receive the transmission at the same time once they tune in with the right frequency or channel.

I would not doubt if our minds work similarly. This view may be contentious to many Christians. But as we are all members of the 'body of Christ'; as we are hid with Him in God (Colossians 3:3,4); there is no doubt we shall all receive from Him as He transmits to us all. Remember too, the parable of the vine and the branches (John 15).

If we continue with this analogy of transmitting and receiving, we find that different sets, radio or television, play out the information to us with varying clarity. Similarly, each of us transmit our ideas differently depending upon our values, standards, and belief-systems. If the examples I now bring to you are relevant because you can understand what I am saying clearly, then my views will have some meaning to you. If they are in harmony with your life experiences, then you will agree with me.

This meaning and agreement we experience in communications contribute to personal magnetism. Even voting practices prove this truth to some extent. We feel comfortable with persons of similar ideas and views. We enjoy fraternizing with like minds. Nations in our world form one economic or political body because of common interests. Trade unions reach out for solidarity nationwide, scientists share research data, accountants form associations and so do other professionals—all because of common interests. For these commonalities are the essence of true bonding.

No two persons are alike—even when they are 'identical twins'. We have to learn to recognize our differences and to co-exist with tolerance. The human forces of attraction and repulsion in relationships are true. To continually study and realize them will only help us to better cope and be patient and cooperative with one another. In this way, guilt and regret will often be strangers to us all.

Belief and Knowledge

Should our conscience be trained to function on the strength of what we believe or with what we know? The Bible tells us to believe and to know many things. There must obviously be a difference between these two actions. What is this difference? Which of these should we put into our conscience? Belief or knowledge? Should both groups go simply because the Bible tells us so?

Psalms 119 says we should lay up God's words into our hearts, meditate and reflect upon them. The psalms is telling us here to trust in God and His precepts. The Psalmist obviously must know what he is talking about. He must have definitely proven that to meditate and reflect on God's words have benefits. It is no wonder why he sings praises to God in this psalms, for he knew of God's power and majesty. Yet there is no indication whether he *believed* in God or *knew* of His Almighty power first.

The Bible, however, says that we should 'Test everything. Hold on to the good' (1 Thessalonians 5:21). This command is clear and tells us we must know first before we act upon any preachment. Here the Bible excludes the dreamers and the believers. It appears to support the persons with scientific philosophies as well as pragmatic practitioners. One may say that Jesus contradicts this when he said 'For God so loved the world that he gave his one and only Son, that whoever believes in him shall not perish but have eternal life' (John 3:16). For here we are expected to believe and accept what Jesus said without proof. But Jesus has shown time and again that his methods are consistent with proof first, then belief.

He could have simply answered John the Baptist's disciples saying that he, Jesus, was the saviour and redeemer written of in the scriptures. Instead, he told them to tell John that the sick was healed, the lame was made to walk and the blind can now see (John 15). Thus to answer John's question of 'who Jesus was', Jesus used his proven deeds which John could have corroborated with the scriptural prophesies. For only the one who can do the things Jesus did was the saviour and redeemer the scriptures spoke of.

What is the difference between believing and knowing? Of what value is this difference to us, if any at all?

King Jehosohaphat said to the people of Judah and Jerusalem, "Listen to me, O Judah and inhabitants of Jerusalem! Believe in the Lord your God and you will be established. Believe in his prophets." (2 Chronicles 20:20, *NRSV*). Jesus answered his disciple Peter on the question of prayers and belief by saying, "Therefore I tell you, whatever you ask for in prayer, believe that you have received it, and it will be yours" (St. Mark 11:24).

In both these examples above, and in many others that we see in the Holy Bible, we recognize that to believe is to trust without a material and objective basis for doing so. This kind of belief is called blind acceptance. It is a trust based on a personal conviction that the Bible is God's word. It is a trust validated on the acceptance as fact that Jesus is the son of God and that he is God incarnate in human form or that he was of divine origin.

In this sense, the act of believing is to adopt the mind set of a child as he or she trusts and obeys a parent. This child mind-set suggests a dependent state. It is saying that for any belief, we are wilfully giving up our power to decide and to choose; we are sacrificing our right to reason or even think things through before accepting any conclusion. We are subjecting our reasoning powers to an authority figure or system we accept as greater than our own.

Beliefs are significant to how we regard people, things, and experiences. Our beliefs become divisions on our inner measuring rods: our conscience. We make assessments and judgments on their strengths. If a principle, idea, or behaviour is in discord to our beliefs, we judge negatively against the discordant conditions or situations we encounter.

We like or dislike according to our beliefs. In fact, many of our values and standards are formed by them. Our beliefs further form the foundation of our self image; that is, how we see ourselves. They are the pillars that make us feel good or bad about ourselves. If they are shaken and we realize that they are unsound, we can feel very bad and have a negative self-image. On the other hand, sound bases for our beliefs will give us healthy self-esteem. It is therefore vital that our beliefs are not based on wild assumptions or dogmatic pronouncements.

Our knowledge, on the other hand, has been tried and tested. Our life experience has borne them out to be true. When we know 'something' we affirm we have had a personal relationship with that 'something'. We can attest to some kind of intimacy, such as a direct interaction with qualities of that 'something'. Thus our knowledge means we are familiar with the object we claim to know. We acquainted ourselves with the sense data arising from our personal interaction with the object.

Belief is like knowledge in the sense that we react to both of them similarly. They both consist of principles which we impose on our conscience. They both are used as foundation pillars when we build our houses of values and standards. We also develop confidence and conviction from our beliefs and knowledge. Therefore, as stated, they are important to our self-esteem and self-image.

Still, they are different. While our mind set, as we have said, for our beliefs, is like a child's; for our knowledge, it is like an adult's. With knowledge, we reason. We do not give up our power to decide and the use of our own will. With beliefs we take whatever was given, as it was presented. While in knowledge, we pick and choose: we screen, then select and so decide what becomes knowledge by virtue of our applied logic, reason, and proof.

By picking and choosing we do not mean that we decide we shall know this point or principle and not another; rather, we are saying that when we know something or have knowledge about it, we mean that we are conscious of it. That is, we have personally witnessed that the something is true or real. We logically and with reason test and try what we accept until it has a reasonable meaning to us. This then is how we know.

In a general sense, any interaction between our minds with objective, subjective, or subliminal conditions constitutes a personal and intimate experience for ourselves. Now the truths, principles, and the lessons we learn herein, are what we call knowledge. After all, we have seen each at work in our daily lives. We remember their causes and the effects. For the results were either pleasurable or painful.

If in the future we are confronted with the possible recurrence of these experiences, we already know the outcomes. Thus our conscience will signal us based on our memorized knowledge.

Perhaps, it is at this point, we should consider the difference between **actualities** and **realities**. The former is the nature of existences by themselves, whilst the latter, refers to existences relative to us. The English philosopher, Bertrand Russell, called these **realities** and **appearances**. To clarify these terminologies: what we have called actualities, Russell called realities; and what we have called realities, he called appearances. For example, an object existing by itself of which we are unaware, we say it exists in its ***actual state***, while Russell says that the object is *real*. But when we do become aware of it, we say that the object is now a ***reality*** to us, while Russell says the object has an *appearance* relative to us. Regardless of terminology, at our point of reality or Russell's appearance, we know the object and we put it into our knowledge banks.

This type of thinking helps us to conclude that we learn from our experiences in life. Whether these are objective, subjective, or subconscious (spiritual). Once we have intimately or personally interacted, then we have experienced. For instance, if we see, hear, or touch an object, we have objectively experienced it. If we thought of it, reflected upon it, we have subjectively experienced it. If we have a vision, a dream, or hear the whispering of the Holy Spirit; then we have subconsciously or spiritually experienced a subliminal reality. Since we come out of all experience aware of our interactions as well as with associated emotional reactions as pleasing or displeasing, such awareness constitutes knowledge.

The problem we often have is when we confuse the two meanings. We use the words belief and knowledge interchangeably and so with time we do not recognize the differences. What we think is knowledge is often belief; but as we have accepted it as fact and true, we argue that it is knowledge. The mere acceptance of a fact does not make it knowledge for us. This is belief. It is only when we begin to examine our views and ideas; when we begin asking how and why we have them, that we frequently experience doubt and uncertainty. For what we think we know, we do not understand why we say we know it. This makes us feel uncomfortable. Especially when another person questions us about our claims or views and we cannot properly answer them. We begin to feel insecure and even foolish as doubts are created in our minds.

Are we really sure what we believe is true? How do we know that the convictions we have are true? Is it because we cannot explain them to another, that we have no knowledge of them; that is, no knowledge of the soundness of our views? What is or can be a self-test that our views are what we know rather than what we believe?

Some things are easier to prove than others. For instance, what you are reading now is a book. With this, one might easily agree. Then again, there are somethings we may not be able to prove to another at all, like the cool breeze we might feel when we sit to meditate on God's glory. Why bother to prove to others anyway, you might ask? At least we should be able to find someway to convince ourselves that we know rather than believe. Not being facetious, but such a discovery may help us keep our sanity. Anyway, it would be important if we can find a way to discern our beliefs from our knowledge.

Discernment is a very tricky process. We can fool ourselves. The Bible says, "A rich man may be wise in his own eyes, but a poor man who has discernment sees through him" (Proverbs 28:11). When we are involved in an experience, we are actually receiving vibrations and impressions which interact with our consciousness and are then interpreted by our minds. This is called perception.

Science teaches us how we perceive when an object is outside of ourselves. For instance, light rays hit the object, then bounce off the object and hit our eyes. These rays, which incident upon our eyes, create impulses that travel through our nervous system to our brain for interpretation. At this point, we see the object.

In a subjective experience, one can speculate that it would happen very much in the same way: except that it all happens mentally. In reflection, we use memory. We direct our attention using our will to focus on specific thoughts, ideas, or views within our memory banks. Our judgment and reasoning faculties will be active in this process of reflection or contemplation. It is during contemplation that ideas and thoughts harmonize or make sense to us and become points of knowledge. It appears that what we actually do is to compare and contrast these ideas mentally and then confer values upon the syntheses. Whatever makes sense we understand. It has meaning to us and therefore is knowledge.

Biblically speaking, spiritual experience has very little to do with our own will. Except, as many persons feel, the part our will plays is to decide to let go of our inner operations. This occurs when we begin to seek spiritual knowledge. Letting go allows another initiator or driver, our subconscious mind and will to take over and bring into our being whatever the Almighty desires.

We may argue this as much as we like; but the fact remains, we do not will a spiritual vision, dream, or whisperings from the Holy Spirit. This last we may call a revelation. Note the revelation of Daniel, Joel, and in the Book of Acts we are told that by means of the Holy Spirit we will all be able have dreams, visions, and all kinds of revelations (Daniel 2:28; Joel 2:28-29; Acts 2:16-18).

We cannot really prove our beliefs to be true unless we develop suppositions and then find conclusions that are factual. From these facts we may now by inductive reasoning contend that our beliefs must also be true.

Although with some forms of knowledge, we may often find it difficult to prove to another, we nevertheless remain convinced and are strong at heart. Our positions are held by a stonewall attitude: we are almost immovable. Our finding explanations too is easier. For we will be talking about our personal realities—that which is real to us. No one dares to challenge our personal truths. Such presumptuous action is ridiculous.

Once we experience in our own lives the wonderful workings of our Creator through prayers and meditations, we know God exists. We know that we are 'hid with Christ in God'. We know that we have risen above the cancer and ugliness of this world and we are one with our Creator as Christ Jesus was in oneness or in harmony with the Father by regularly praying, doing God's Will, and maintaining a righteous behaviour and character.

If our beliefs are sound and our knowledge are not delusions, but universal truths put into our hearts, into our conscience; when our conscience says 'no' or 'yes', we have our Lord's disapproval or approval and curses or blessings following our intentions, thoughts, and actions.

Collective Conscience

The Holy Bible says that God destroyed Sodom and Gomorrah (Genesis 19:23-26) because "The outcry against Sodom and Gomorrah [was] so great and their sin so grievous…." He went down to see if what they were doing "…[was] as bad as the outcry that [had] reached [Him]. If not, [He] will know" (Genesis 18:20). Here the Bible speaks of the *'sin of the cities'* as if the cities are one entity. That is, the cities were treated like one personality with a seared conscience that persisted in its sinful and unrighteous ways. We know that the *'sin of the cities'* referred to is the sum total of the sins or the *collective sins* of the inhabitants of the cities. Notice when the two strange men arrived into the city, the people taunted Lot to send them out so that the citizens can have sex with the strangers. The people (both young and old from all parts of the city) shouted out to Lot, before the family went to bed saying, "…where are the men who came to you tonight? Bring them out to us so that we can have sex with them" (Genesis 19:4-5).

Prior to the strangers' arrival into the cities of Sodom and Gomorrah, Abraham pleaded with God to show mercy on the righteous—his nephew who lived within the city walls of Sodom. Abraham repeatedly asked God if He would destroy the righteous along with the wicked and God responded showing his love, compassion, and mercy for humanity. The Bible says, God is " a gracious and compassionate God, slow to anger and abounding in love…" (Jonah 4:2). In fact, God said He would not destroy the city of Sodom if he had found at least 10 righteous amongst them (Gen. 18:23-33). Once again the city has been treated as having a personality of its own. The collective righteous behaviour of a group is judged on behalf of the entire city.

What we can learn here from this dialogue is that there can be hope and salvation in situations that may appear hopeless. Here God is willing to save Sodom if he would see a significant sign of righteous behaviour amidst the despicable characteristics. Individuals who may appear hopeless to us, may have some redeeming qualities that the Lord sees, and which we cannot, and so they receive salvation. Remember to the prophet Samuel, by the appearance of Jesse's first son Eliab, the prophet Samuel thought that Eliab would be the most suitable to be the king of Israel after Saul. But God 'sees the heart whilst man looks on the outer appearance' (1 Sam. 16:6, 7). The little and apparently insignificant looking last son, David, was God's choice to be the next worthy king of Israel. Note too that Jonah felt the people of Nineveh should have been destroyed by God for their sinful ways; but God saved them (Jonah 3:10; 4:1). God is most merciful and sees people and conditions different from us.

With respect to the city of Nineveh, the king received the word of the Lord and he commanded his people to fast and repent. The people showed remorse for their violence and vile conduct and God did not destroy them—despite the desires and wishes of the prophet Jonah who felt they should have been destroyed. It took the collective attitude of penitence, the entire city's participation in fasting and prayer for the city of Nineveh to be spared by God. Notice too the change in the city's heart and wicked ways had the cooperation and full support of its leadership. It was the king and the nobles who made a public degree to fast and to cease the wickedness and disobedience of divine laws. The cities of Sodom and Gomorrah with its fate reminds us of the unrepentant way of King Saul who was destroyed; while the city of Nineveh reminds us King David who repented and was saved.

No matter where we live or in what century we were born, each soul personality traverses through life, as it learns the lessons it needs and acquires the knowledge and wisdom necessary for its evolution. With a penitent heart, the Bible shows that each soul personality is then bound for a mystic journey called the Christian Walk. After fighting the good fight and finishing the race, it is ready for salvation and the gift of the crown of righteousness (2 Ti. 4:8). Its rises and falls, its successes and failures are determined by the degree of its obedience to the training and retraining of its conscience (James 1:22-25). As it is with each soul personality, so it is with each family, organization, country, region, and the world. In the case of a group, the quality of its findings and outcomes is determined by the collective conscience of its members. Let us remember the Biblical examples above: Sodom and Gomorrah and Nineveh.

In an earlier chapter, we saw that the scriptures discussed four classes of conscience: strong, clear, weak, and seared. We also discussed the overall behaviour of each class: the strong, determined to be guided by God's word; the clear, feeling no remorse as the soul personality complied with its righteous dictates; the weak, due to ignorance, irresolution, and inexperience yields to temptation; and the seared, reacts in accord to its immoral, unethical, and derogatory values.

We are now looking at an aggregate of consciousness, a group of beings treated as one, a unit—having its own conscience with values established by some form of consensus or unanimous agreement. The Bible also speaks of judgement against the following cities— Ammon, Moab, Edom, Philistia, Tyrus, and Zidon (Eze. 25-28). These cities have all been treated as collective personalities. Their inhabitants sinned against God and He punished them. Had any repented, as did Nineveh, God would have pardoned them.

A country's heritage and culture, its people's rights and freedoms, its form of government, its constitution and legal system all make up the composite qualities of its global population. Any act or speech made by any province, state, city, or citizen that is contrary to its established laws, rights, freedoms, and beliefs, will be condemned and be labelled as treason. Such a *treason* is a '*sin*' against one's country. For it is such an action that is evaluated and measured against those standards accepted by the country—an act violating the values and the conscience of the country.

Just as our individual actions are judged against the standards, rules, morals we placed into our hearts and conscience, so too are the acts by organizations in our societies measured against our country's laws and culture. This evaluation process is also seen when nations violate rules of conduct established for the world by the United Nations' mandate to which they agreed. The consequences today may come in the form of economic sanctions by the United Nations. We may say therefore that a country has a social conscience, similar to that of an individual.

Let us look at a group of say fifty person forming an organization, all of whom agreed upon a set of rules and regulations as well as a specified list of objectives. We can safely say that depending upon the kind of contribution to their society or nation, they will, as a group, be respected or disrespected, honoured or dishonoured. We have seen how the principles, practices, and beliefs of political organizations in power, have caused them favourable or unfavourable responses: they are either voted back or out of office.

This assessment of an organization as a group is true for all bodies: whether they are business, political parties, religious, or otherwise. If this kind of judgment is true for a group of ten or fifty members, then it must be true even for one of twenty-six million or five billion. After all, organizations with millions of members are either countries or large international societies with a list of commonalities: beliefs, standards, values and so on. Today it is popular to talk of worldviews. For instance, the Christian worldview would define all those characteristics, values, and beliefs that are Biblically based and held by the believers.

Earlier, we saw that conscience is an indicator which signals when we are right or wrong in the face of our own values and standards. It is not really a judge—conferring right and wrong value judgments on our deeds and thoughts; but a watchman or better an alarm system. It is not religious or righteous; but mechanical in its operations. Our conscience simply just is.

Conscience is a loyal, devoted, and impartial servant, whose function is simply acceptance or rejection after receiving impressions, and checking them against established standards. If, as a political party, we fail to act in the interest of the public and therefore in discord to the laws, beliefs, and precedents we knowingly and publicly agreed to, we would be voted out of office by the citizens.

This concept of an aggregate consciousness or a collection of objects viewed as a single entity is not new at all. For as Christians, each of us is unique and separate; but we are all part of the one and single body of Christ. Paul said to the Colossians, "For you died, and your life is now hidden with Christ in God" (Colossians 3:3). Also, Jesus tells the parable of the vine and its branches in John 15. The life sap the vine absorbs from the soil will be given equally and totally to all the branches. Here too, is the concept of composite existence— hence collective consciousness and conscience.

Surely as Christ is the vine and we are the branches, we are one with Him. And as He is in oneness with the Father, then so are we. We look at nature in our cosmological proof of God's existence. Let us look at the oneness of all earthly waters, the oneness of the air on earth, the oneness of the soil. We replicate it in electricity, in TV and Radio stations.

It is indeed a wonderful realization to discover that with our acceptance of Christ, we are in one with God Almighty. Further, as the parable clearly illustrates, if we are out of harmony with Christ, that is, if we are a rotten branch, we will be severed like the operation of a surgeon cutting out a malignant growth from our bodies. It is much the same way we treat unwanted characteristics or behaviour in our society.

As the Noah and the Sodom and Gomorrah stories illustrate, it was the wickedness of the people in the lands that brought about their destruction. If the stories of the lost and sunken cities of Atlantis and Lumeria are true, then perhaps they too had a compensatory end as they may have fallen victims to the material and fleshy pleasures. Or perhaps there were issues of pride or the improper use of knowledge. For those who consider Plato's account of Atlantis allegorical, then let it be so to them. Their consideration and any other, their discounting Plato's truth does not in any way affect the idea presented here regarding group conscience, personality, and character.

As a family, Noah, his wife, his sons, and his daughters-in-law, survived the destruction by the great floods when God was displeased with "...how great [human's] wickedness on the earth had become, and that every inclination of the thoughts of his heart was only evil all the time" (Genesis 6:5). Note human here refers to the human race—a collection of *homo sapiens* or human beings. Noah's family was righteous in the eyes of God. As a unit, their group behaviour and conduct was in accordance to God's universal and divine principles of love, fairness, and mercy. Despite the condemnation and ridicule by their neighbours when their consciences sanctioned their obedience to God, they continued to build the Ark in the middle of the land, far away from the sea. In the end, their obedience and their strong conscience saved only their lives.

We should not be surprised when we hear heads of states, government ministers and county councillors encouraging their citizens and people to rise up as a community to correct or improve conditions. Everyone knows that we are accountable as community members and citizens of a country for our welfare and progress. For instance, if the citizens of the country become more aggressive, more creative, and more self-reliant, then more persons will initiate projects, become self-employed which may greatly alleviate the unemployment and other economic burdens that plague the society. I only mention this as an example of an individual's community spirit and accountability, not as the solution to the present economic state of the world.

The admonitions and urgings by these leaders emphasize not just the sufferings of the organization or society, but that the responsibility is on the shoulders of every individual of the society to resolve the social problems. They, therefore, foster social awareness which in its truest form deals with the collective concern and attention given to conditions affecting everyone in the neighbourhood. The law of each being his brother's keeper must be fulfilled (2 Pet. 1:5-7).

When we improve our laws and ground our legislature in humanitarian causes, giving greater freedoms to self expression and stimulating greater justice, mercy, and brotherly kindliness, we are building a social and collective conscience that will be in harmony with God and His universal love.

The words: mankind, society, state, province, county, region, and world, connote the uniting of smaller and independent units to form a larger whole. Hence each group with its individual values, beliefs, ideologies, and other qualities, is a unit in itself with total sensitivity and responsivity to situations and conditions existing outside and inside itself.

All these composite units sit in an ocean of consciousness. They are united because they sit in this unbroken mass of sensitivity and responsivity; though separated because of their statements, their actions, and their reactions are as individual bodies.

The popular cliché 'Birds of a same feather, flock together' is a universal acknowledgement of collective conscience. Many people today still assess another by the company the latter keeps. Parents are guilty of demonstrating this type of assessment. And when their children get into trouble and perhaps is not longer performing well at school, the parents blames everything on the attitudes and behaviour of their children's companions—especially when these companions often get into trouble.

Not always, every individual in a group agrees with the group's decision and action. Take a look at the democratic process: we have the right and freedom to vote whom we want to govern us, and the majority wins. If we are not in the majority, then our exercising that right did not get us the person we would like to see in office. Yet we must obey the Laws and Acts this new government legislates. Our individual views do not represent the body or community of which we are a part. Further, we have to acknowledge and accept our community's rules despite our disapproval. And if we are law officers, we must enforce them.

Within the democratic process, we can protest the parliamentary enactments with which we disagree. And as has been seen in our societies, if we make enough noise, if we gather much support, we may affect the laws by influencing the inclusion of new subsections and modifications. This procedure is similar to what we do with our own values. When we discover a better way, we reason and justify and finally change our views. Changes may not occur every time and as quickly as we have stated here; but each small effort contributes in the long run for any minute difference or improvement in our overall system. Every effort is valuable to the whole.

We must treasure our freedom to vote and to run for public office as citizens. This right proves that each of us can affect the overall direction of our societies. This right also means that each is culpable equally for the quality of the output. Because of this, each of us is accountable for whatever type of conscience our society collectively displays.

Changing Morals

When the apostle Paul went to Athens and was asked by the Epicurean and Stoic philosophers to speak at the Areopagus (the Council or Court), he did not start his address saying, "People of Athens, I am going to inform you about the one and only true God." They may have kicked him out of town, because of gods, they had many (Acts 17:16). Instead, Paul wittingly and wisely praised them for their interest in new ideas and for how religious they were. He continued to note that they paid the greatest homage to one on which they inscribed "AN UNKNOWN GOD." Paul said that was the very God he represented (17:23). Naturally much curiosity was peaked and he concluded with the gaining of some converts. For what he said changed their values, perceptions, and beliefs. The Bible says, "A few men became followers of Paul and believed. Among them was Dionysius, a member of the Aeropagus, also a woman named Damaris..." (Acts 17:34).

Surely there were those who sneered, and that is to be expected (Acts 17:32). Change does not come easily. There is usually some resistance. It has always been a dilemma in human experience. We are comfortable where we are because we are familiar with the conditions about us. As soon as new conditions step in, we feel uneasy—even when these conditions are for the better. After we have adjusted, we are pleased with the change we have had.

But why do we often feel so unsettled about changes? Is the fear or anxiety we feel due to a negative prejudgment that the new condition may not be agreeable? Or is it due to an inherent laziness which vexes because we must make an effort to adjust and shuffle? These may seem ridiculous questions; but when we think of our behaviour regarding changes, we quickly realize that we cling to familiar surroundings as if with them is our only way of surviving. For changes scare us.

In Isaac Newton's first law of motion, he says that objects remain in the same state of rest unless acted upon by some external force. So if a box sits on the table, it will remain there until we lift, push, or pull it. Or we may move the table or a strong wind may blow the box off the table. If we roll a ball in one direction, the same law applies. Gravity, friction, wind, obstruction, or some other manifested push or pull can cause it to change direction or stop.

Since the box and ball, according to Particle Physics, is a mass of vibrations, then their overall vibratory rates must be constant while they remain in any position they are in: fixed or moving. Also, all forces and pressures without and within them are balanced as they remain in their positions of rest or motion.

We, too, are made up of substances. The laws of motion must also be applicable to us—even including our behaviours and thoughts. After all, our thoughts are vibratory. If they were not, we would not be able to realize them. Our behaviours are subjects of our thoughts, and the former depends on the latter.

Now when a force is applied on an object, we know a change occurs—no matter how small. This change is a new vibratory rate and condition in nature of the object. It must naturally affect the nature of the other vibrations with which the object interacts as the object's weight or the friction between itself and the surface on which it rests. Just think of the effects of repainting or remodelling our house, or the cleaning out of our chest of drawers. Everything is scattered and disarranged from our first action until we are done. In the end we have an arrangement that is constant for a time. All the different items are now in place. A new order has been set up. At last, stability has returned.

We have grown so accustomed to constancy that we see chaos as disruptive, negative, and unwanted. But recent scientific views of the universe includes a new perception of cosmological behaviour called the chaos theory. Whether in the years to come, this theory becomes law or not, today we have a distaste for any chaotic condition. We have always linked the change-process with chaos; for the obvious reason that chaos is defined by Webster's Dictionary as "utter confusion and the absence of form or order." This, at first, is exactly how we see changes. In a sense, what we do not understand is chaotic. Understanding leads to clarity and meaning.

Any change implies movement. That is, a kind of displacement— progressing from one place to the next. Whether this displacement is in time or in space makes no difference to us: we still show restraint in dealing with it. Regarding time, we are conscious for a period of one reality, and then another; with space, we are first in a familiar location, and then in an unfamiliar one. These two types of experiences of displacement or change have the same kind of effect on us: hesitation.

We hesitate, not simply because we are unsure of what to do, but because we are afraid that the outcome may be bad or unpleasant. If we know that the outcome will be pleasurable, we will not hesitate. It is when we face the unknown we become afraid. One may say it is lack of faith or lack of courage. But it is neither.

Lack of faith suggests that because of intuitive foreknowledge we should have known the outcome would either be good or bad for us. When there is an absence of faith, doubt steps in. But doubt always shirks conviction. This is indeed a religious view. Mystically speaking, if there is intuitive confirmation of a future change, there will be no fear—as this expected new state will be self-evident to us. We will feel an inner conviction and confidence about the goodness of our expectation. Lack of courage, however, may usher an adventuresome attitude—though there may be fear because of existing or anticipated dangers. Whenever we are determined to investigate and or conquer the adversities, we demonstrate the constitution of which our heroes are made.

Our fear of the unknown stems from our self preservation instinct. We seem to have the innate desire to continue our existence—as we know it. This impetus to always be is central to the condition we call "life." It also appears that because of this impetus, we have the drive to eat, sleep, and carry out all activities essential to sustain this life. Thus any event that may appear to threaten life, we tend to avoid.

If this impetus in life did not exist, we would not need to fear any event: new, dangerous, or unknown. But this is not the case. Fear is a necessary indicator that a discordant situation is present. This oncoming threat could mean the end of our existence or death. Thus our egos react emotionally with avoidance, discomfort, and any other obstructive behaviour to changes.

Though unknowns may be good or bad, our egos being aware of their presence, always put on its self preservation armour. It seems always we expect the negative and not the positive. Perhaps this is so because we know so little of what is within and around us. Thus the possibility of errors in judgment and discernment is greater. It is no wonder the scriptures say, "…my people are destroyed from lack of knowledge" (Hosea 4:6).

The conditions of shock, surprise, difference, and uniqueness are all experiences of change. We are in one state that is stable and familiar, and then gradually or suddenly we are aware of another new set of conditions about us. We went from a 'now' followed by a 'then' realization. In other words, we traversed in our consciousness through a continuum of occurrences. The final unfamiliarity of which we become cognizant constitutes new elements of experience: new images, new sensations, new ideas.

This interaction between our consciousness and actualities is inevitable in life. It is the reason we know. While we are awake, our interaction with existences is continuous. We can see here, interdependence. It would seem like the central theme of life is action. This in human terms is behaviour. When this behaviour generates pleasant or unpleasant feelings, we call the former group of feelings good or right; the latter, bad or wrong.

Now all the good and likeable feelings we repeat and continue to look for ways to improve them. If the pleasure we derived from the last is better than the previous, we have discovered a new and higher value for good; similarly, we have different values for bad. Naturally, most of us feel what is good is right, and what is bad is wrong. As life progresses, we continue to have many experiences and so the groups of rights and wrongs we call morals. Let us remember that not all our morals are derived from pleasant experiences, but painful ones too.

Our successes and failures in life depend on these morals. New morals that give us more pleasure is indeed a change from the old. We may conclude that our greatest pleasures would come from changing our behaviour to be in harmony with the highest expression of good we know. Though we desire to experience these pleasures subjectively, we must also mentally strive to harmonize with the highest good we can conceive. We may further speculate that a similar behaviour is required for us to experience spiritual pleasures—the ones found in the consciousness of Christ when we become part of his body: our conduct must be in tune with divine decrees.

Perhaps the greatest change that we can make in our lives, and one that is sanctified by God is when we give up our old life and begin to live the new one. Romans 6:2-11, in the Holy Bible tells us once we have accepted Christ Jesus, once we have been baptized in the name of the Father, the Son, and the Holy Ghost, we have died and resurrected with our Lord Jesus. Paul went on explaining in Romans 6, the difference between the old and the new life. He said of this wondrous change, we will reap the benefit of holiness and eventually have eternal life. The question is, how can we interpret these scriptures into the language and the meaning of life today?

At one Bible study meeting, a sister asked, "Why do we have to wait for all these blessings when we are dead and buried?" She obviously finds that once we have accepted Christ, we should be having and seeing some benefits right here on earth. We sometimes do. Many converts talk of how much their lives have changed—and for the better. Some reported how much new difficulties they encounter from the time they have accepted Christ as Lord of their lives. Those who persist because they knew their faith was tested later assure us that it was worth it; others quit with regret.

Many would agree with our beloved sister that we should have our blessings now—not later. After all, in Ecclesiastes Solomon says we can only praise God and enjoy life when we are alive. We should not hesitate to act and lose precious time. We can do nothing when we are dead (Eccl.9:5, 9, 10). In Matthew 6:33, Jesus said that we must "seek God's kingdom and his righteousness and all these things will be given to you as well." When we seek God's kingdom, and this is to accept Christ, we definitely will have eternal life. Christ promises here that God will take care of our needs today as well, though the entering his Kingdom we will experience that not in this life.

But this life of eternity comes after we have completed our earthly lessons. It is futuristic. We are not wrong in asking, "What about now—right here on earth?" Our loving and merciful God has promised that not only will we receive the eternal life after death at his final judging; but that while we are alive, we will have other blessings and benedictions.

For Jesus has said that "all these things will be given to you as well." The sister is right. God is truly a wonderful God. For when Jesus said, "all these things," he was referring to material things and benefits. We will see this when we read the entire chapter of Matthew 6.

Simply changing our ways and stop doing the ugly, sinful acts of yesterdays, simply obeying God and not following in Cain's footsteps, is to have salvation and to open the floodgates of heavens, of blessings from God. Our God has undoubtedly provided bountifully for those who will follow and obey him.

When we pay our tithes and offerings, he will open the floodgates of heaven for us (Malachi 3:10); when we pray and believe we'll receive our desires, we get it (St. Mark 11:24); when we sow, we reap (Galatians 6:7). All these promises are fulfilled right here on earth, on this material plain of existence. For in heaven we will not need these blessings anyway.

The process to begin changing our life is a simple one. Just to say "Yes! O yes, I love Christ Jesus. Yes, He is Lord. Yes, I am hid with him in God. Yes, I shall lay my burdens on him. Yes, I shall yoke myself with him." This is all that we need do to change and begin the wonderful process of growth. But we must mean it too.

The word change, however, is clear in its meaning and implication. It means to convert; that is, to become different. It implies that we are now something that we were not. It implies movement from before to now, from old to new. Maybe, the newness might not be unique, but it would be different for us. The morals we had we no longer have. The thoughts we had we no longer think of. We cast the "old man"—that old life—away.

What was this old life? What did it consist of? What are the kinds of things we use to do? In Colossians 3:5-8, Paul said that in order for us to have holy lives, we must get rid of our old nature by putting to death the following: "sexual immorality, impurity, lust, evil desires and greed, which is idolatry." And with regards to our character he said we must "rid ourselves of anger, rage, malice, slander, and filthy language from..." our lips. We must analyze ourselves and as Paul continues "Get rid of every bitterness, rage and anger, brawling and slander, along with every form of malice (Ephesians 4:31).

Paul did not stop there, for he told us the qualities we must now clothe ourselves with: "compassion, kindness, humility, gentleness, and patience." He continued talking about forgiving our brothers and most of all put on love which binds all the above virtues.

The apostle Peter also spoke of the kind of qualities we should have when we put on the new life and accept Christ. In 2 Peter 1:1-5, Peter said,"...make every effort to add to your faith, goodness; and to goodness, knowledge; and to knowledge, self-control; and to self-control, perseverance; and to perseverance, godliness; and to godliness, brotherly kindness; and to brotherly kindness, love." Also, the apostle Paul said that we must "Be kind and compassionate to one another, forgiving each other, just as in Christ God forgave..." (Ephesians 5:1).

It is obvious that to change from the old to the new life is to know the difference between right and wrong. "The wrong" is the way that leads to eternal death and even unhappiness in this life; whilst "the right" is the way that causes us to reap "all the other things" that Almighty God will add in his love and in accordance with his promise (Matthew 6:33). The issues dealing with right and wrong acts are moral ones.

To many, what feels good is right and what feels bad is wrong. But as stated earlier, the Bible clearly spells out both wrong and right acts. We may ask then, what of those issues that are not clearly stated in the scriptures that we may be involved in, how are we to determine right from wrong? There is usually a scripture in God's word that will apply, if not specifically so, then in principle. After all, there is wisdom in the divine plan and creation of man. God gave us intelligence and access to universal wisdom and collective consciousness in the "body of Christ."

The highest good that Aristotle talks of is when a deed is good in the eyes of society. This view is also in the Holy Scriptures. In 2 Corinthians 8:21, the Bible says, "For we are taking pains to do what is right, not only in the eyes of the Lord but also in the eyes of men." So a good measuring rod is to compare our action with the good of society—provided that such action does not in any way conflict with how Almighty God generally tells us to behave as an individual and as a group. Here is where we look at the "spirit of the laws" of God. This is indeed a matter of Grace. If humanity approves but God disapproves, then our action is wrong.

Often an act may hurt us not because it is wrong, but because we have come to love the evil ways or we simply have a misinterpretation or delusion of the truth. Change to us becomes hard as most of our old behaviour has become habits with which we are comfortable.

Habits are the laws of our being, as stated by the wise and the illumined. By regularly carrying out any type of behaviour it becomes part of our nature and almost an involuntary action. This means, they are burnt into our consciousness, into our hearts, and minds. They become part of our value and judgement system.

Therefore, if we develop bad or wrongful habits, then our conscience would not torment us when we enact them. Unless of course, in a "blessed moment of silence," the Holy Spirit whispers to us and we feel guilty and know, despite a well established habit, what we intended doing or have done was indeed wrong. For those reasons, we must ensure that we adopt the right behaviour—ensuring at all times to keep such behaviour in line with the Scriptures.

Eyes of Understanding

To say that our understanding has eyes is literally misleading. Eyes are for seeing—for recognizing and identifying. When we see, we receive light rays in our eyes that bounce off the object we will soon recognize or have a picture of at the end of the process called vision. These rays then hit the sensors on the retina of the eyes causing impulses that travel along the nerves to the brain. There different sensations are created and the images are formed thus making a duplicate of the object actually outside of us. It is our brain which then interprets this image. If our memory has the image recorded, we recognize what we see or we conclude it resembles some object we already know—otherwise this image we will now add to our mental library records.

Many of us respond when explanations are given by saying, "I see." What we really mean is "I understand." We say, "I see" because "to see" means "to recognize" and it is simpler and shorter to say than "I understand" during a conversation. Besides, "I see" is commonly used in English conversations. Novelists use this sentence regularly. It is almost used like a fad or slang. Here then when we say, "I see," we mean "I know what you mean" or "I understand what you are telling me."

Now understanding is a subjective experience. It is not a faculty nor is it knowledge or wisdom; rather, it is a stage before the realization of knowledge. It is the focal point where "relevance" and "meaning" dwell. It is where there is harmony and accord between our conscious attention and sense data in our minds.

When we understand a thing, condition, or situation, we mean that all the facts, elements of knowledge, or different thoughts, are put together, thus culminating into a unit or whole. In basic chemistry, we learn that a single atom of oxygen cannot exist by itself: it is unstable. It must exist in a pair. However, it can also be stable, when the single oxygen atom combines with two hydrogen atoms to produce water: a stable substance. Another analogy is with pieces of a puzzle forming a flower. No one piece of the puzzle makes sense or resemble anything we know or can recognize; but when put together, they have meaning to us: we affirm it is a flower. Our understanding works in a similar manner.

Memory is invaluable to understanding. Either we have the bits and pieces to put together or we receive them from some other source. No matter from where they come, all the bits and pieces, when assembled, must resemble something with which we are familiar. Usually much of the bits and pieces contributing to our understanding is stored in our memory.

Understanding is certainly not an object with qualities of substance that we can perceive with our physical senses. It is an occurrence, an effect. It occurs before recognition. One might even argue that understanding and recognition happen almost simultaneously; for at the point we understand, we recognize, providing the event is familiar to us. We can also arrive at understanding through logic and reason. Here what we understand may not resemble any object or condition we already know. Thus what we understand is probable or possible.

In the first instance, the moment all the puzzle pieces are put together, a specific, distinguishable pattern results: an understanding with which we are accustomed. But there is always a base, a connecting bridge, or a point of reference. We cannot go from, for instance, basic mathematics to advanced in a moment, unless the gap between is filled. This gap or void is filled with new facts and information that forms the link between the current arrangement of our sense data and the point where they become sensible.

From a philosophical point of view, since the substance of our memory is consciousness which is like a stream of water with different objects floating on its surface; then understanding is like any meaningful arrangement, shape or pattern of objects that was brought about by the various currents in the water. Let the objects be the facts; the water, the consciousness, and the current be the mind-force inciting combination and interrelation.

You might ask then, what of those aspects of knowledge that makes sense to us but not to another and no matter how hard we try, we just cannot prove it to them? This situation is similar in a sense to the one wherein we arrive at probabilities and possibilities through logic and reason. In both instances when events are merely possible or probable and when we do not understand, we are in a realm of unfamiliarity. The vibrations, sensations, and feelings may not be entirely new; however, their arrangement may be.

When we arrive at our conclusions rationally, and providing our assumptions were correct, then our doubt is only due to our unfamiliarity and our inability to relate our findings to what we already know. And in the instances that we just do not understand, no matter the explanations we receive, it is because the gap between our current experiences and what is presented to us is wide. Thus it is difficult to relate the new and unknown to the known.

We need time. We need a period during which our conscious mind can adjust and become familiar with each stage of information from the familiar in our memories to the new. In this period, we will be gradually discovering relationships and recognizing connections. Thus our awareness is expanding. It stands to reason that patience and tolerance must be a quality of those who are already familiar with the novel occurrence.

If the principle of memory is vital to the process of our mundane experiences of understanding, then it must be the same in the spiritual realm. Those who religiously disagree with the aphorism "As above, so below," must remember when Christ was teaching the disciples how to pray (Matthew 6:9-13), he said, "…your will be done on earth as it is in heaven…." I remember immediately the concepts of macroeconomics and microeconomics. The words macrocosm and microcosm also come to mind. Further, the basic principles of managing a home or a business are the same as those to manage a country. This is simplifying things a lot, but I am concerned here with principles. In any case, I have never heard of a university course on "How To Manage a Country." Perhaps it would be a good idea to have one considering how many are run. I personally am unqualified, but I can say as a citizen of the world, such a course is needed. Thank goodness for the democratic process wherein we have, as citizens, the ability to cause a change in leadership and how our countries are run.

As Christians, we want to live the life Christ lived—using his behaviour as a model. Of course, we are not talking about being crucified to save the world. That job has already been taken and done. We do not have the capacity for it anyway. That work was ordained for Jesus the Christ. We are only humbly asking to copy the path he took to the fullness of our own little capacities. Who can really match the work of the Christ in such exactness? No one. Notwithstanding the obvious axiom that each of us is unique, it has been said of all the avatars, he is the greatest; of all the sons of God, he is the purest; of all the souls, he is supreme and Godlike for unto him "…every knee shall bow and tongue confess that he is Lord" (Phil. 2:2-5).

For when we are in Christ, neither the natural nor the carnal man is in control; but the spiritual man. Therefore we cannot sin. We want to hide ourselves with Christ. We want to be the branches as he is the vine. All these hopes which we say we realize with redemption by his blood means being perfect in Christ.

What Christ is, we are; but not in the fullness of who and what he is. We continue to strive to grow towards that fullness. A soul must be prepared in character, traits, fortitude, love and absolute submission to the will and wishes of God the Father and in precise unison with the Holy Spirit. Christ's kingdom is ours for he conquered death and once we follow him then we too are conquerors of death. He has authority over all principalities and so do we, through him. The aphorism, "As above, so below" is alive in the life of the true Christian. Therefore, if there is memory in the consciousness of Christ and in God, such divine memory and universal records has all infinite principles and laws. Our submission and surrender to Christ as he is now absorbed in the consciousness of God means that we will be one with him. He always obeyed God and said that his Father's will is his, and he is one with the Father. To submit ourselves to God is to unify with his consciousness and thus have access to his divine memory. Certainly just as each light bulb connected to an electrical circuitry, shines in brilliance to the capacity of its wattage; so too each of us in unison with the consciousness of Christ is illumined to the capacity of and degree of our submission and worthiness.

When our spiritual or mystical experiences are realities to us, it means that our sincere submission and trust in our God has granted us access to his divine wisdom and font of knowledge. That is the formula: submission (child-like attitude) plus total trust (faith) joined by sincere desire (our choice to fear the Lord) will automatically bring us the reward of salvation and eternal life. Our understanding of divine laws, principles, and how God's kingdom functions will grow and this is one of the blessings after the formula is applied.

The eyes of understanding is the principle that is responsible for our realizing anything. It is not a faculty or a thing; but the means by which we enjoy and know life's existences, conditions, operations: be they subliminal or mundane.

It is a fallacy to think we can deepen, improve, develop, or increase our understanding. We often talk of having a "greater" or "better" understanding of a subject. I know this is a contentious statement; but what we really mean is that we have gathered additional facts, more sense data and so we therefore have acquired a fuller or a more comprehensive picture or viewpoint. This means only that our knowledge or realization has increased. The facts and sense data were always present; we only, at a later time, were able to fit them in the large picture.

It should be clear that understanding is invaluable to our conscience. For conscience needs understanding to process spiritual and objective data. The more we understand, the more data we assimilate, is the greater our realization. Hence the sounder and more reliable is the voice of our conscience.

The psalmist said, "I gain understanding from your precepts; therefore I hate every wrong path" (Psalm 119:104). Precepts are rules of conduct, maxims. When the Psalmist became aware of them, God's will and wishes became clearer to him. His life must have had greater meaning. For he can obey God's commands knowing the benefits and blessings he will derive. As what he gained was clarity and knowledge of how things interrelate. He knew then what to accept and what to reject that is the reason he said he hates "…every wrong path" (Psalm 119:104). The psalmist also knew the penalties of his wrong actions.

Earlier, in a few verses before this one, the very psalmist said, "Oh how I love your law! I meditate on it all day long" (Psalm 119:97). Here we are clearly told that if we regularly read God's words; if we let it be absorbed into the core of our being, it will become alive in us. For it will then be a part of us. Surely the psalmist benefited by complying with the law: no wonder he loved it and read it daily. Eventually, such a law will become part of ones being due to familiarity by habitual use.

When we confront any situation, we will evaluate it with these precepts—these rules of right and wrong that we are accustomed to and are in accordance with the will of God. All the facts of the situation, will enter our consciousness wherein is already stored our highest standards. The more we learn of God's laws, the closer will these standards come to be more perfect reflections of divine principles. Time and growth improve our vision for truth, our eyes of understanding.

Discerning Spirits

In our encounters in life, we hear many voices telling us what to do or what not to do. These voices usually do no agree on any issue. For each presents a different course to take. What is obvious is that no matter how many alternatives presented in any situation, there can only be two options for each alternative: yes or no. What remains is to identify the true source of each voice and to determine the soundness and truthfulness of its counsels.

The theme of a message one of my pastors once preached was "Fearing God." He went on to explain that throughout the scriptures, the word fear was used more than one hundred and fifty times. He said that fear carried two different meanings depending upon where and how it is used in the scriptures.

There are times, he said, when we must tremble in the fear of the Lord—those are times when we receive his wrath and anger because of our wrong actions. The other times, he said, fearing God meant to respect and reverence him. Upon close examination, we note that these two meanings of fear relate respectively to disobedience and obedience. For there is no reason to be afraid of a God who is loving and merciful, unless of course, our behaviour is out of harmony with his expectations and laws. Once we know that we are obedient to His will and wishes, we are at peace and our consciences are clear. But if we are disobedient, we would be tormented within and live with the fear of being recipients of the wrath of God.

For example, Adam was given specific instructions. God told him what he must not do and what he can and should do; but a voice, a spirit—outside or inside himself—spoke and Adam listened which led to his condemnation and the loss of his divine birthright.

Throughout life, we are faced with two options in every decision. After our selection, we now must decide how and when to carry it out. Our life's greatest successes and failures are hinged on our right choices, our correct discernments. One may wonder why, after having chosen the most appropriate course of action, we should hesitate in our decision to implement it. This wonder addresses the core of the enigma called disobedience.

From an intellectual standpoint, we have thoroughly and rationally analyzed the pros and cons. But there may still be is hesitation: a subtle resistance to carry out our own intelligent decision. This may be due to another voice telling us all that can go wrong if we pursue our intended course of action. Thus the impetus now needed for implementation is not there. This means that all the complementary factors to initiate action will also be absent. So a rational, logical conclusion, our decision may just feel wrong.

Why? What is the setback? What force could oppose our reason and logic? What could defy our entire thinking and intelligible processes to make us feel hesitant; and yes, feel threatened, guilty, or doubtful?

We know our conscience can object to normal reason. But at times even when we draw conclusions based upon our highest morals and conceptions of good—the stock of which our conscience are made—our heart is still irresolute. It seems that we occasionally experience an inner sensing and knowing that we are wrong. This uncertainty is an interruption of our individual cognitive processes as well as of our conscience. For we can only have self-doubt when our inner self becomes aware of knowledge beyond the domains of our personal memory, judgment faculties and conscience.

As a trained Christian Educator, I can attribute our vacillation to the presence of the Holy Spirit bringing with it an influx of new knowledge and wisdom to our attention and for our consideration. Some may say that we have tapped, at that point, into our subconscious resources or a higher consciousness and mind. By whatever name this "divine source that interrupts" is called, we have to deal with yet another option which imbues our consciousness as self-evident. Again, which 'voice', which 'spirit' do we listen to? How can we discern rightly and then decide to materialize our choice?

In the Holy Bible, God said that Adam and Eve were no longer ignorant souls after they had experienced the taste of the tree of knowledge—they now, like the angels know the difference between good and evil (Genesis 3:22). Humans now possess the ability to recognize the duality of all existence—right from wrong.

They had not, however, developed the habit of doing right. For, they first learned greed and disobedience (Genesis 3:6). The Bible says, "When the woman saw that the fruit of the tree was good for food and pleasing to the eye, and also desirable for gaining wisdom, she took some and ate it. She also gave some to her husband, who was with her, and he ate it."

Second, they learned to instigate another to do wrong (Genesis 3:6). Eve "…gave some to her husband…, and he ate it" (3:6). Further, God said to Adam, "…you listened to your wife and ate from the tree about which I commanded you" not to ear (3:7).

Thirdly, they learned shame (Genesis 3:7). Note the Bible says, "…they realised they were naked; so they sewed fig leaves together and made coverings for themselves" (3:7) Then we read that "…the man and his wife" heard God in the garden and hid from Him because they were naked (3:8).

Fourthly, they learned guilt (Genesis 3:8,10). Adam was afraid because he was naked and did not want God—the creator—to see him. He should felt free and uninhibited in the presence of his creator. No restriction in his heart, nor created walls and prisons of decency, should make him hide from God.

The fifth wrong quality humans learned was self-justification and "passing the buck"; that is, blaming another instead of being accountable (Genesis 3:12,13). Here the Bible did not mean to be facetious, but we chuckle disgustingly when we read Eve blaming the Devil for her own wrong doing saying, "the serpent deceived me, and I ate [disobeyed you God]" (3:13). Earlier Adam blamed his wife Eve saying, "the woman you put here with me—she gave me some fruit from the tree, and I ate it." But notice how Adam even went further in *classical implicative language*, using the intelligence God gave him, wittingly blaming God for his own sin: it was not just any woman who persuaded me God, it was the one—that one which You God gave me. We may extend it and emphasize for clarity that Adam means, if you God did not give that specific woman to me, I would have NEVER sinned.

It is further clear that it was vanity in the heart of Eve that caused her to yield to the "satanic promptings and voices" she heard. For satan told Eve that "...God knows that when you eat of..." the forbidden tree, "...your eyes will be opened, and you will be like God, knowing good and evil" (Genesis 3:4-5). This appealed to Eve, so she sinned by disobeying God's decree. She succumbed to her vanity (Genesis 3:6). Of course it was Satan who nudged her to sin. But he played upon the vanity he discerned in her. After all, Satan did not force Eve, she made the choice to disobey and so she is full accountable for that major role she splayed in the dram of "the fall of humanity."

Let us note that neither Adam nor Eve showed any remorse or regret. They never repented nor asked forgiveness of God. We can speculate as much as we like that if they had repented and asked God's forgiveness, perhaps the outcome of the relationship between God and humanity would be different. Life would not have been as challenging as it is today. But we cannot waste time speculating for "the dice had already been cast" and we have to just deal with the reality of "the fall" and be grateful to God's loving and merciful redemptive plan—our path back to a sacred romance with our creator.

Both of Adam and Eve had to deal with the problem of discernment. There were many "voices" in Eden as there are in our lives today: God's, Satan's, conscience, the objective-reasoning mind, other individual's. Discernment was indeed confounding from the beginning. It still is. Many people have much to advise when others have relationship problems—or any kind of problem for that matter.

Not all suggestions are constructive. Some are motivated by jealousy, others based on individuals' personal and varied experiences and values. What we must do is listen, weigh, reason, and move to a place of quiet and ask God. He commands us, "Be still and know that I am God" (Ps. 46:10). It is in this *silence in which we enter*, in this transcendent state of meditation, within which our Lord speaks truths to us. For a moment herein our souls are illumined.

We are not surprised to see Paul's concern that his fellow Philippians when he said to them in a letter that he was praying that their love "…may abound more and more in knowledge and depth of insight, so that [they] may be able to discern what is best and may be pure and blameless until the day of Christ…" (Philippians 1:9-10).

Since Adam was brought down by his yielding to Satan, it has been spiritual warfare on earth. In Ephesians 6:10-17, Paul tells us that we are fighting not against flesh and blood, but against spiritual wickedness. But God Almighty loves the world and therefore wants us to return to him (1 Timothy 2:3-4) and have all the blessings and benedictions that Adam first had. He, therefore, designed a plan and gave up or sacrificed the life of his beloved Son, Jesus (John 3:16). For it is only through accepting Christ, by flooding ourselves or hiding in his consciousness, can we ever hope to earn salvation and be redeemed (1 Corinthians 4:12).

Peter, in Matthew 16:22, said to his master and messiah that he would not allow his master's enemies to kill Jesus. But Christ said, "Get behind me Satan, you are a stumbling block." Now we know that Peter loved his master, and he did not mean to keep or hinder him from his mission of saving the world. We also know that Peter was not Satan. But the evil one, Satan, uses anyone, anywhere, anytime. From our best friend's lips we may hear the counsels that will cause us to stumble.

The Bible also said, do not trust her who lies in your embrace (Micah 7:5). The Bible is not encouraging enmity between spouses. It is just another example of the wiles and ploys of Satan to create confusion and dissention. Remember Job's wife? During Job's pinnacle of showing his love, devotion, and faithfulness to God, as Satan tests

Job's loyalty to God, Job's wife said, "Are you still holding on to your integrity? Curse God and die" (Job 2:9). She could not stand to see her husband suffer so much. And with that, we all might agree. However, Job knew that a larger and more eternal price was at stake here: we must have faith in God—even in times of trouble (Job 2:10)

We must remember that Paul said we are not fighting against flesh and blood but principalities. Thus Christ did not mean that his beloved Peter was attempting to make him stumble; for he knows how the enemy functions. So too we must not despise our loved ones and friends for obstructing us. We must be tolerant and know that it is not the persons themselves but their obstructive counsels we must avoid.

The Bible teaches us what comes out of a man's mouth defies him (James 3:1-12). We are to check what we say to another before actually doing so. For the same tongue or mouth that praises is the one that curses (James 3:10). Here there are two areas of accountability: one arises from what the speaker says, and the other, from what is understood by the listener. It is the responsibility of the speakers to articulate as precisely as possible the meanings they intended to convey and leaving as little as possible or ideally no incorrect interpretations.

The Bible tells us to take care of what we do so that it may not cause another of weaker conscience to stumble. For to hurt another (be it a brother, sister, or stranger) in such a way as to cause them to sin is to sin against the divine consciousness and will of Christ (1 Corinthians 8). These admonitions urge us to be cautious of what we say or do. Note that as we cause another to stumble, and we sin against the consciousness of Christ, we also bring upon ourselves a punishment for our misdeeds in accord to the law of compensation.

Whatever prompts our action and speech must always be evaluated. The Bible tells us in 1 John 4:1, that we must try and test the spirit even if it is of God's. We have to be aware of false teachings and false prophets say Jude (Jude 1) and Peter (2 Peter 2). Not only must we be cautious in listening to any individual's suggestions; but also of those invisible entities whose truthfulness we cannot determine.

When we dream or have a vision or are intuitively prompted to say or do something, we must thoroughly assess the idea or thought—no matter who said it. After all, God himself has said that we must test his spirit (1 John 4:1), and that we must always prove or verify the soundness of any principle or belief (1 Thessalonians 5:21), to ensure that what the source gave us is correct in the eyes of the Lord.

God has given us the freedom to choose and act in the way that pleases us. He also instructed us about the consequence of our actions as well. Paul said that "...each one should carry his own load" (Galatians 6:5). Therefore, we are all accountable for what we say and do. We will not be pardoned by blaming someone else as Adam who blamed Eve and she then blamed satan (Genesis 3:12-13). All three paid the price, received their just compensation for the part they played in violating a command of God (Genesis 3:14-19).

Adam said to God, "...it was the woman you gave me that cause me to sin" as though he was ignorant of what was wrong and was thus easily deluded. Many of us try to hide behind the wall of ignorance and say we did not know and expect sympathy and pardon. God has said in Hosea 4:6, "...my people are destroyed from lack of knowledge." Ignorance is not a valid reason or excuse for sins, breaches, crimes, or disobedience of any kind.

God, because of his love, intelligence, justice and mercy, gave us a way to ensure we do not fall victim to eternal damnation. He gave us His word, the Holy Scriptures and He told us in 2 Timothy 3:16, that "All scripture is God-breathed and is useful for teaching, rebuking, correcting, and training in righteousness."

He also told us that we must in our actions seek not only to please Him, God Almighty, but to please our brother and sisters (2 Corinthians 8:21). Jesus has shown us, among the many instructions and guidelines He taught the world, that whatever we do, we must do it to glorify the Father. Christ said, "My Father,...may your will be done" (Matthew 26:39). We have also been given the Holy Spirit, the comforter. Christ said he would send him (Jn. 15:26). It is the Holy Spirit who imbues us and causes us to prophesy, dram, have visions, revelations and wisdom (Joel 2:28, 29). This is yet another means by which we are guided to do the right thing.

We conclude, therefore, that the scriptures show us how to check our thoughts, ideas, intuitions, dreams, and visions to see if they are of God. First we must check to see if the action or utterance inspired or implied is consistent with the Holy Scriptures. Secondly, we must do a bit of possibility testing by asking ourselves, what if we do or say it, what then.

Here we must see if we may truthfully hurt another. I say truthfully as there are many times that we are right and it may hurt another but we must continue as no sinner will be pleased by the righteous action of another. Thirdly, we must assess our intent to determine if we are helping our brother or sister in a constructive way that will benefit them truly. Fourthly, we must not take such action to cause anyone to stumble or to sin. And finally, we must be certain, absolutely certain that God is glorified, not ourselves.

Too many voices are in our mind sometimes. As stated in Micah 7, we must not even trust the person sleeping beside us. This is tough; but the Christian path is a tough path. We must remember though that it is not the person we are up against, but what they say or do to hinder us. We "struggle" says Paul, "not against flesh and blood, but against the rulers, against the authorities, against the powers of this dark world and against the spiritual forces of evil in the heavenly realms"(Eph. 6:12). Was it not Job's wife who was telling him to curse God when he was suffering and lost many of his riches and the lives of his children; and his four close friends, in spite of their sincerity, misunderstood his trials and therefore gave him wrong counsels?

We have all, at one time or another, been victim of the good intentions of friends and family when they provide us with advice based on their misinterpretation of our circumstances. At the same time, our reason and logic present us with a different view in which we had no confidence; and a soft voice whispering to us a feasible option—though comprehensive—seemed unimportant to the loud, pounding, and popular conclusions.

Empty vessels indeed do make the most noise. Yet which voice to listen to? This question we must forever repeat to help us remember that many will always knock at our door. This way we will remember how to identify each voice and finally elect them by rightful discernment: the one to which we must submit.

Trials and Tribulations

Saul's troubles and suffering were not trials; they were tribulations. The Bible says, the Holy Spirit left him and God sent an evil spirit to plague him (1 Samuel 16:14). Because of Saul's sinful acts, he lost favour in God's sight. We pointed out earlier that he never repented nor asked God's forgiveness, according to the records in the Bible, and so his accounting for his deeds was severe. His conscience made him restless. It clawed away at him like an invisible being seeking revenge for all the wickedness and injustice it suffered.

To some extent, many of us have had a similar experience to Saul's. We reluctantly or never show regret for our sinful actions and therefore we drive the Holy Spirit from our presence; that is, we become out of harmony with the oneness and consciousness of Christ. Our feeling no remorse demands from God's universal laws that we pay dearly as if hunted by an evil spirit sent to compensate us in accordance with divine law.

Saul was anointed by God to be king of Israel (1 Samuel 11:15). He was approved and elected by his righteous conduct and by the Israelite's choice. As the Lord's anointed, he was more so obliged to live righteously. The Holy Bible repeatedly illustrates that if we do not comply with God's commands, we pay with the hope that we will learn the needed universal principle for our growth and awakening. This is not a punitive system at all; but one of progressive discipline, to use human resources management terminology. God wants us all to be saved (Rom. 11:26). He loves us all and gave us a way back to friendship with Him (Jn. 3:16). If, despite the warnings from our conscience and God's revelations, we persist in our evil ways, we will create for ourselves a sure pit of hell. This describes King Saul's downfall.

David, a beloved servant of God, was in no way initially a more perfect person than Saul. In fact, David's adultery with Uriah's wife brought him the wrath of God. He lost the child he was about to have; but he repented and once again caused the Holy Spirit to return in his presence and he later triumphed. Saul, we observe, did not repent, so he died everlastingly.

When we sincerely repent our evil deeds, we actuate another law: the law of mercy. Truly our God is a God of love and justice. He seeks every way possible to save our souls. Even though he knows of our fallibility, he ensures that our burdens are of a weight that we can bear (1 Corinthians 10:13). It is not that he set our tribulations before us; but that he knows, when we are compensating for our sins, we are emotionally, intellectually, and spiritually ready to learn the lessons from our errors. Still, like a student in a class who refuses to pay attention and who has a need for the same lesson to be repeated; we find that in life, we too may have the same hurt repeated until we have no more need to learn the principle associated.

What then is the difference between trial and tribulation? The one is a test and a blessing; and the other, a punishment. Trial gives a pain that strengthens; tribulations, a pain that tortures. One is a crucifixion with Christ; the other, the incarceration of the soul by hell fire. Trials we thank God for, as they build character; tribulations, we must plead repenting for redemption.

Experience shows that throughout our journey in life, we encounter different situations primarily by choice. Accidents, fortunate or unfortunate circumstances occur by our unconscious choices. This does not mean that when we are asleep we choose; but that we are often unaware of the result a particular election may cause.

This ignorance of the final occurrences of our choices and the laws they actuate are what we call accidents, fortunate or unfortunate circumstances. Our other encounters may be initiated by no immediate act or choosing on our part, but by our worthiness and readiness to go a step further in our development. These last occurrences are called trials or opportunities. If we run counter to our conscience in these, we have to account. By the pain and suffering we feel, we will know we have activated impartial and effective laws for our learning.

This pain we feel for trials and tribulations are the same. Its intentions are the same. Both conditions are unbearable. Both tell us that something is wrong. Pain is an effect or signal: a consequence of disharmonious interaction. It is neither good nor evil. Yet no normal person likes it. We all want it to go away—and fast. For this reason some feel it is evil: because it conjures in our minds negative thoughts, and because of the discomfort we feel.

Since the beginning, all that God dislikes in man, He makes clear. He was angry at Adam's disobedience in eating the forbidden fruit (Genesis 3:17). He cautioned Cain about his downcast look and jealousy because these feelings may lead him to sin (Genesis 4:6-7) which they eventually did. For Cain later killed his brother, Abel (Genesis 4:8). God also grieved because of the wicked acts and inclinations of the human race (Genesis 6:5-6).

Because of our sins, God decreed that we must labour to eat; that women will bear child with pain; that there will be perpetual spiritual warfare between Satan and humanity (Genesis 3).

Labour, child-bearing pain, spiritual warfare, and banishment from our Holy inheritance, are all conditions associated with discomfort. They are all punishment. They are all painful. And when we suffer from stress as we labour to achieve our goals in life, we experience discomfort too. It is no wonder we often confuse both trials and tribulations: both carries with them much stress, worry, and frustration.

Everything that is good and desirable to the normal man is painless. We always strive for the easiest way out, for the shortest route, or for the path of least resistance. By nature, we avoid work and pain as if they were fatal diseases.

These tendencies are directly in opposition to God's first commands that we must eat by the sweat of our brows and bear children with pain. Even the apostle Peter said that if we are to reap God's kingdom and his blessings, we must expect fiery trials in the Christian walk (1 Peter 4:12). We cannot escape the woes ordained by God: fiery trials lead to God's blessings; sins lead to punishment.

The adversity we feel in a worthy task is due to our own insecurity, lack of faith, and our being out of attunement with the love of Christ. If we truly know the infallibility of God and trust in Him, place our burdens upon Him, much fear, worry, and restlessness in our lives would be absent (Matthew 11:28-30).

Are not all our worries over eventually? Look back at them a moment! Even though we agree intellectually, it is no easy task to demonstrate and live a life of full conviction. After all, Christ, before he was taken by his enemies in the garden of Gethsemane, kneeled and began asking God if He could take the cup and burden away. But notice later, his burdens ended and he sat in glory on the right hand of God, "the Mighty One" (Mark 14:62).

Every pain and joy soon passes away. Nothing lasts forever. Our experiences in life prove this repeatedly; but the misery and torment from pain always seem to blank our memory. Thus we forget that our present hurt will pass away. For in Ecclesiastes, Solomon said that everything is for a season.

Perhaps one reason for our blank memory or momentary forgetfulness is due to our disobedience of daily reading the scriptures. For regular repetition of any act is conscientious practice. And by practising consistently, we develop habits which become part of our involuntary consciousness. So when we are suffering, our subconscious mind will stimulate our memory to bring to the centre of our conscious mind the scriptures: this too will pass away.

Though our hurt will not disappear, the worry that accompanies it would. For the Bible tells us when we cry to the Lord for help in our troubles, God will deliver us from our distress (Psalms 107:28). It is our worrying that intensifies our pain, much more than the actual condition causing it.

Take Moses for instance in the beginning of his mission when God spoke to him (Exodus 3 & 4). Fear and doubt in confronting the elders of Israel and the Pharaoh of Egypt caused him to be overanxious. He did not feel he was competent enough to do the job, which the Bible shows he had done with excellence. Moses did not know that God only gives us to bear what He knows we can carry (1 Corinthians 10:13).

This truth also applies in the case of Jesus's mission. As Jesus felt the agony of his crucifixion in the garden of Gethsemane, he thereafter had inner peace as he realized the dependability of the Father and His Laws. Jesus said, "My Father, if it is not possible for this cup to be taken away unless I drink it, may your will be done" (Matthew 26:42). He was worried although he was not actually on the cross as yet. Clearly from this quotation, we see that as soon as Jesus expressed his doubt and hesitation with regards to his fulfilling his life's mission, he had an immediate *inner conviction* following which he regained his fortitude and composure to do the Father's Will. But we all would agree that Jesus already knew the truth and had full knowledge of his duties and its implications (Lk. 2: 34, 35; 49Jn. 5:36, 37). Yet he needed the counsellor—the Holy Spirit to comfort him.

But Jesus has always been an obedient Son. For the Bible tells us that every spare moment he had he went to a private place and pray and communicate with the Father (Luke 18:1-8). God also spoke to Peter, James, and John the brother of James about Jesus and said, "This is my Son,…with him I am well pleased" (Matthew 17:5).

It is plausible that what happened in Gethsemane, was as soon as Jesus felt weak and asked God to take the "cup" away from him, God's Spirit must have consoled him; for he said, "…not what I will, but what you will" (Mark 14:36). He has regained his strength. The spiritual man in him is once again in control. For Jesus knew his mission was ordained, necessary, must be accomplished. Yet he asked God, "…if it is possible for this cup to be taken away." The implication here in Matthew 26:42 is that Christ had to complete his mission so that God's plan could go into effect (1 Peter 1:18-21). His use of the word "possible" shows that he knew the need for a "perfect" *ransom* or *satisfaction* to mitigate what the first Adam had done by separating humanity from God in the fall (1 Cor. 6:20; Matt. 20:28; Mk. 10:45).

Therefore, despite the excruciating pain on the cross, Jesus asked God to forgive mankind as they did not understand the fullness of their action (Luke 23:34). We know that Jesus did no wrong; for Judas confessed that he had caused innocent blood to flow (Matthew 27:3-4). It was God's will for Jesus to fulfil his mission. It was Christ's acceptance and choice to give his life. In a similar sense, many of us suffer in a Christ-like manner: when we do humanitarian work—glorifying God (1 Peter 4:13). Of course, we do not suffer to the degree that Jesus the Christ did—even those who were martyred.

Since Christ did not bring the burdens he bore upon himself as did the two thieves who were crucified besides him, his "cross" was not a tribulation, but a trial. Moreover, he could have given up on each occasion he was tempted: after his fast in the wilderness, or when Peter uttered *stumbling* remarks to him about his mission, or at the moment he cried before his capture. The option to refuse to fulfil his mission was always open, just as it is with each of us.

But at his level of mastership and spiritual development, there is **only one law, one way, one choice**: obedience and submission to the will and wishes of God. For he said in the end, Father, not my, but your will be done.

In the Old Testament, David repented regularly and showed great reverence for God. No matter how often he sinned, he would always ask God's forgiveness. He also took his punishment responsibly—knowing that he sinned and was therefore accountable. He did not "pass the buck" as Adam did.

When the prophet Nathan came and rebuked David for his sin against Uriah and his adultery with Bathsheba, Uriah's wife, David did not deny his wrong. He repented, fasted, and suffered the consequences (2 Samuel 12). He did not say it was Bathsheba's fault because she had no right to bathe in the nude where he could see her from the top of his palace. Instead, he accepted accountability and compensated fully.

Job, too, was a very loyal servant of God who throughout his suffering never gave up his love and loyalty to God. He humbly kept his communication with God daily. He cried out to his Lord for deliverance and he eventually had it; as would we, if we emulate Job's example. No friend nor wife could shirk him in his love to submit to his God or to 'cop out' of any trial to which he was subjected and which was approved by God. He met the challenges of his trials, not with his intelligence and indomitable spirit, but with self-denial and self reliance best described as absolute surrender and submission to God. He knew that in the end he can depend on God and he was prepared to die rather than disobey God.

The apostle Paul talked of the value and responsibility we have in serving the Lord. He even spoke of the trials we must be prepared to suffer and talked about the crown of righteousness we will receive in the end of our Christian Walk. Paul too was prepared to die in the service of our Lord. He felt that his duty to fulfil his life's mission as he suffered trials was the law and order of his life—the reason for his very existence.

When the shadows come into our lives, we must remember personalities like David, Job, and Paul. We must think of even Saul too—as we should keep in mind the penalty of immoral, sinful behaviour. For we should also know what we ought not to do.

When our conscience bothers us we know why. We must have said or done something discordant with our standards. We feel like the Holy Spirit has left us—not that it has gone elsewhere—but that we have cloaked ourselves with a cloud of darkness by our evil and immoral ways that now blocks out the lustre of God's love and His Holy presence.

Trials in the name of God we seek and we can only endure by being yoked with Christ; tribulations, when they come—as they will, we battle with a feeling of remorse and with sincere repenting. We must ask God for his forgiveness and thereafter live and act in fear of Him as we train our conscience (Hebrews 5:12-14).

Puzzle with Obedience

Just as faith without works is dead, so is conscience without obedience. For as faith is immaterial—having no physical and substantive composition; so is conscience, an existence that is also intangible. The works of faith and the obedience of conscience must always glorify God and benefit mankind.

What is this experience called obedience? Why has it been such an enigma to people? Does it simply involve the action of saying "yes"? If so, why do we find it so difficult to do? Does it go against our true nature? What is our true nature anyway? Has disobedience to do with right and wrong; that is, morals?

Since the beginning of time, humans have had a problem with the phenomenon called obedience. Spiritually, we know it has caused our greatest downfall. Still today, we are constantly plagued by the effects of our first disobedience. These effects, we do not want, yet we continue to cause them by our wilful thought and action. One may think in this sense we are inherently self-destructive or foolish.

From the youngest child, when given instructions, we see early signs of resistance to obedience in the form of indiscretion. To the adult on the job or in society, when told about the work rules and the social laws, we have an inward prompting of discordance as we may even momentarily feel these rules and laws threaten the sovereignty of our free will. But how free is this free will? Is there a limit to our freedom and power to choose? Or is this resistance in us prompted by the "old self," that sinful nature with which we were born—the one inherited from Adam's sin?

It would seem that our lives are flooded with the scrap from our disobedience. The amount of pain, suffering, anguish, and frustration we experience as an aftermath of our interaction with the world, our fellowmen, and our own inner urges, we are certainly poor deciders.

We often fail at cooperating with nature's laws too. We receive pleasant or unpleasant responses depending upon what we say or do in situations. Some of these responses are lasting while others are only for a short time. The pleasant ones we like to have go on for as long as possible; yet we persist in our illicit activities that bring us the suffering we do not want and often find unbearable.

When a child obeys what his parent directs, he is loved and appraised as wonderful and beautiful. Even the praise of being "a God child or a blessed child" is conferred upon him. Whether or not the directive was consistent with divine laws or basic morals at the time is not the issue. At least the directive would be in harmony with the will and wishes of his parents. Thus the child was obedient.

Obedience deals with whether or not the person complies with the will of authority figure and or systems, rulers, heads of organizations, laws of society, the organization's doctrines or dogmas, constitution and statues, or God's will. Further, the person must be aware of his contrary actions, because he was directly instructed about "do's" and "don'ts"; or regulations that he should know.

Do we need only be a follower to be obedient? Can we think for ourselves or should we simply do as we are told? If being obedient is this simple, why is it a dilemma for man?

In attempting an answer to these questions, we must first define or explain the nature of obedience. It is an expression. The mere discordant or accordant thinking does not constitute disobedience or obedience. Obedience must be expressed in words or in actions. Its activity must be compliant with the current standards used to determine whether or not it is obedience. Obedience is a kind of submissive behaviour; that is, it is the yielding of one's own will and choice. If our values are in accord with the person directing us, or the regulations with which we must obey, then we experience no compulsion to obey.

It is our right to think for ourselves and also our right to fight for this freedom. Our destinies should lie in our own choosing. Since we are ultimately accountable for our actions, then we must at all times reserve and maintain our power to choose. To choose to obey must be supported by our own, individual conscience—not forced upon us nor put before us as persons incapable of thinking for ourselves.

We like to please ourselves: to do and say the things that gives us physical, emotional, intellectual, or spiritual pleasure. Any decision which goes counter to our values and standards, will in our own estimation, cause us displeasure; so we avoid them. They seem as if they are forced upon us—violating our right to self-determination.

At this point we do not care about right or wrong; but only with what is or is not pleasing to our own egos. If the principle we disobey can cause us penalty or reward, our disobedience will bring much suffering. Many stories in the Bible illustrates this clearly. The dramatic affair with Adam comes to mind.

But we have no different nature from him. Even when we read and re-read the holy scriptures so that it should prevent us from sin, we often go astray. This is because what we have read and studied has not really scarred our conscience nor made an indelible impression in our active memories.

Conscience is like a valve in the continuum of our life activities. It is a preventative maintenance program set up by Almighty God—a life-long control and monitoring system to help us keep on the righteous track. Once we place God's words in our hearts, in our conscience, and we act, conscience clicks in, signalling right or wrong behaviour—even intention. When we go contrary to it, we disobey.

Conscience is inside of us telling us to save ourselves so that we will have benefits here on earth as well as eternal life after our transition. Since we are not born with the awareness of the words of God in our hearts, then those absolute virtues we manifest are not really our creation.

From birth, we have been trained to listen and develop the fleshy parts of our beings. Truth for us is defined and appraised through the physical mind and our intellectual desires. Spiritual desires always tend to seek the benefits of others and glorify our Lord. Selfish qualities do not thrive in the spiritual man. It is these two worlds of desires that are in constant warfare in us. It matters not that we split selfish into natural and carnal. The principle still applies.

Obedience to the spiritual man is hard. We have to train ourselves and keep practising righteousness. This kind of self de-programming requires time, patience, and persistence. As long as we are aware that we are in a constant battle with our own base nature, and it is the spiritual self we should let overcome, we are heading in the right direction. For obedience is the central principle in the affairs of our conscience. Our successes and failures, happiness and sadness, are affected by how we integrate these two.

Whether we find the effect of Adam's fall fair or not, is irrelevant. We cannot honestly deny that we are all prone to disobedience. David said, "Surely I was sinful at birth, sinful from the time my mother conceived me" (Psalm 51:5). After all, despite our divine spirit with its dormant powers and absolute, immortal virtues, the genetic qualities and tendencies we inherit from our parents's imperfect genes must indeed be sinful.

From birth, if we leave a child and not train it properly, it would cry unceasingly; be annoyed whenever it cannot get its own way and grow up unwilling to be cooperative.

When we arrive late for school and work, that too is disobedience to rules and to established expectations. When we eat too much, dance too much, work too hard, pray too much: all these are examples of disobedience. Let us quickly point out that too much praying without action is also dead. Of course, we justify our prayerful excessiveness saying that the purpose is good so we are allowed certain latitudes and exonerations.

But that is not so, for good or godly reasons do not legitimatize the abrogation or violation of any law. God is a consistent God. He said, "I will not violate my covenant or alter what my lips have uttered" (psalm 89:34). Though he will punish our sins with the rod and our iniquities with flogging, he will not stop loving us nor betray his faithfulness (psalm 89:32-33).

Obedience implies compliance to something or someone. In doing so, we must do as we are told or instructed. This does not mean we have to disregard our own will and reasoning in an active way when we obey. Instead, we must use will to be submissive and to yield to the "thing" or person obeyed. We must use our reason to help us "see" that our obedience is sensible and wise. Though full realization of the wisdom to obey may come later, our will to submit to goodness and godliness and our reasoning to sincerely discover the truthfulness of our actions, are supported by an inner conviction—a comprehensive, emotional, and elated confidence that our obedience is right.

Obedience means agreement. Our views matter in a way that we must be desirous to subordinate them to the one presented to us for our compliance. The latter views must prevail. Surely there are two types of attitudes accompanying obedience. One is the feeling that in the act of obeying is an obligation by divine edict; and thus we must show reverence. The other is a feeling of unwillingness because of compulsion due to fear of penalty or punishment.

Our world has had both physical and spiritual growth. Some may disagree as in much preaching is the phrase "in these last days" which is perhaps widely misunderstood. For this phrase has been used by the prophets in the old testament (Joel 2:28-32) and the apostles in the new testament as well (Acts 2:17-21). We must remember that our Lord Jesus has promised that he will pour out his Spirit on all flesh and that greater things will be done. Thus after Christ was gone, many prophesied, healed, and preached—empowered by the Spirit of God (Acts 2).

But do these "last days" refer to the times just before the final coming of "Christ"? Are we not warned of how to prepare to enter God's kingdom? Are they not telling us to ensure we are ready and worthy to enter this divine realm wherein we may reap eternal benefits? And when the Pharisees asked Jesus about the coming of the kingdom of God, "that heavenly, divine realm or state of God," did he not say, "The kingdom of God does not come with your careful observation, nor will people say, 'here it is,' or 'there it is,' because the kingdom of God is within you" (Luke 17:20-21)?

Yet many preachers, as though they hunger for the ending of the universe while they thirst for God's kingdom, they preach with a tongue that interprets a kingdom like an earthly one. This is an open and perhaps, ignorant contradiction to what Jesus said, "My kingdom is not of this world…. But now my kingdom is from another place" (John 18:36).

But many old interpretations are dying or modifying and new ones are born that are more consistent with what the Christ taught. Were it not for the development in our societies in their allowing the freedom of expression, we could not have reached where we are today. Law and Order are greatly modified and becoming more universal. Our world is becoming smaller and more unified through many international organizations and technological advancement. To keep our growth, the generality must comply. Our laws, for instance, must continue to reflect a universal goodness. These laws always carry with them reward and punishment. Comply and be rewarded; violate and be condemned. Obey and be blessed; disobey and be cursed.

It is by our obedience that we will make ourselves worthy for the Holy Ghost to bless us and work through us; while disobedience stains us as the children of Cain.

As a child obeys his father and a servant his master, so too we must obey the one with greater authority over us. Obedience carries with it levels of authority or the existence and setup of graduated levels. The boss pays the salary and provides the job—remember the parable of the Vineyard (Matthew 20:15). The Lord can decide to give the same wage or benefit to the one just working for a day as to the one working for several days. He is the boss, he is the greater, he has the authority, he is Lord.

Our tendency to disobey never leaves us. Even though we know we will be penalized, be expelled, or be condemned, the worst punishment does not deter us. We somehow always feel we can escape; that we are clever enough "to fool the system." Yet during punishment we are unhappy and desperately hope we are pardoned—showing much remorse and regret. But during the times of wrong action we choose to disobey because the action always appeals to us: disobedience always has a nice, sweet taste. Eve saw that the fruit was good, so she ate it.

Earlier we talked of choice and preference. If disobedience is so appealing to us and we often choose it, then it blends and harmonizes with the nature of our inner selves. This "nature" must then be sinful and satiated when wrong acts are committed. We only feel discomfort when our conscience is filled with such values and aspirations that are in discord with conditions confronting us. Reading the scriptures and books that build our morals will be good training for our conscience and so help us along the right path.

What about when we disobey social laws and practices that are immoral? Is this right to do? Though we must give to "Caesar" what is his (Matthew 22:21), Solomon said that our duty in life is to obey God and his commandments (Ecclesiates 12:13). God is greater than "Caesar." We will no doubt suffer for this kind of thinking like Jesus and the apostles did and the many saints that follow who stood for righteous behaviour. Yet we must be thankful for such legislations that grant us the freedom of speech and of religious and spiritual views of our own choosing.

Here, as citizens in a modern world, our constitution and bill of rights allow us the freedom and right to vote or even become electoral candidates—all vehicles to make us agents of social change. Hence we can stand up for what we believe is right by our conscience. In fact, many have made the statement "let your conscience guide you" a popular cliche. While this promotion is positive, we shall examine it closer in a later chapter.

As humans we also know that we are endowed with a free will. This means that we have the authority and power to decide, choose, and act. This power we are born with and so we know we can cause and make a difference. We know too that we can in our societies create; that is, materialize our dreams. All this knowledge gives us much pride and feeling of importance with some degree of self-control and self-direction. To give up these powers often seems to us to lose the true meaning of life and to feel inadequate. But exercising our will makes the statement that "we count." If we use it, not contentiously, but constructively to glorify God and benefit mankind, this then is true obedience to the Holy Scriptures (Ecclesiates 12:13).

Stewards of Earth

Man has been a difficult and stubborn student of life—especially regarding his duty as steward of the earth. He was, by divine selection, put in charge of the plants and animals (Genesis 1:26,28), yet he has always mistreated them and the environment. In his decisions about environmental issues, he often puts his objectives first and the environmental needs last. He hardly thinks of the environment as a partner or cohabitant in the universe. He emphasizes that it must serve him, instead of him trying to harmonize with its forces while he evolves.

When we hide in Christ (Colossians 3:3,4), we become humble, compassionate, charitable, and respectful of all God's creation. We are spiritually awakened and are in oneness with all life forms. We develop a conscience that is overflowing with God's love and laws. Therefore, we must always ask, 'What effects produce ripples or echoes that may hurt other living organisms or cause natural disasters? Do we have alternatives with lesser drastic consequences? By how much and in what way are we disturbing nature's balance?'

For instance, by nomadic practice we give agricultural lands a chance to regain its fertility after harvesting. Or we can help nature by planting grass and breeding cattle or sheep on the harvested lands for a season. Also, we may design houses and office buildings to be built on slopes, instead of destroying the mountains to get flat lands.

We cannot omit conscience from any decision. We must

continually lay up God's words and decrees in our hearts and learn all we can about our co-inhabitants of earth. We must try, as stewards, to live and grow in harmony with all organisms. This is the proof of our realization of the interdependence of life.

For many animals are extinct because they could not adapt to changes on earth. The growth of cities with their industries caused several animals to run and live deeper in the forests. By our continual hunt for treasure, adventure, living spaces, and natural resources, we disturbed virgin lands. We finally invaded the new homes of those animal organisms that escaped to safety in the heart of the jungle.

With industrialization, we pollute our air and water. We have also produced destructive wastes that cost human lives: those wastes manufactures flushed in rivers and oceans. Surely our conscience rebelled, no wonder we poisoned the rivers with nightly dumping and in secrecy. I do not mean that every secret activity is a violation of conscience or of morals or of God's laws. For Nicodemus went to Christ in the night (John 3:2) and Jesus on several occasions commanded people not to tell anyone that he healed them (Mark 7:36). Even companies keep private board meetings. However, the dumping of poisonous wastes into public rivers and oceans is illegal, immoral, and disgusting. This is one private activity that is immoral, wrong, and evil.

The water of many rivers have dried because we cut the trees and vegetation causing rapid evaporations. In some cases, when we completely destroyed mountains with explosives and flatten lands for roads and housing projects, erosion and debris filled the rivers. Today, human lives are also threatened with insufficient food, overcrowding, and energy shortages. The progress of man—his drive to urbanize— has been costly.

The onslaught of developer's efforts to civilize our rapidly growing population and build communities where interdependence can take root and grow, have spoiled and sometimes wiped out virgin forestry. In cities and villages, we feed, clothe, and shelter ourselves by fishing, hunting, agriculture, and their related industries.

The earth's top-soil is quickly losing its fertility because of seasonal and yearly harvesting. The seas and rivers cannot produce enough fishes and other aquatic foods to keep pace with our needs. Nor can the remainder of our forests allow the breeding of enough animals from whose skins we get most of our clothing and from whose bodies we get meat.

This raping and abuse of our environment has threatened and challenged our existence. Instead of finding ways to coexist with nature, we have plundered our surroundings and slaughtered our livestock. With the shortages we caused, we desperately invent, create, and develop alternative supplies and resources. We may have had greater benefits, if we had used our knowledge of our environment to more effectively manage God's creations. But conscience told us so and we did not listen.

Though by divine law, we were naturally selected to be caretakers of planet earth—to be true conservationists, we have become extremists. We let our desires push us selfishly in discord to laws of justice and balance. For pleasure, we shoot birds, hunt and kill much wild animals and fishes. Now out of fear for their extinction, we set up laws to protect the wilds. Somehow, we listen to conscience most when it torments us—not when it whispers.

We do not control our desires, for moderation is hard to live by. In a sense, it is a hurdle we must climb; an obstacle we must overcome. Our conscience has told us to find balance and satisfaction between ourselves and nature. But our personal egos cling to our wants and our selfishness, rather than letting us yield to universal impulses of harmony and balance.

It is an unselfish attitude we need to guide us in moderation when we fish, hunt for food, and bulldoze raw lands. The more we align with the Holy Spirit, the more concern and love we develop for our fellowmen and nature. The Holy Spirit is forever active and whispering truths to us. God has promised to pour His Spirit upon all people (Acts 2:17). It is each person's duty to clear the dirt from his inner ear and obey these divine edicts of love (Acts 2:38,39).

We can neither say nor suggest that the destructions caused by our drive to fulfil our needs and wants are because God did not have a comprehensive creation plan. Let us remember that He is God and is perfect. Let us then examine how unfairly and thoughtlessly we treat one another when we are inconsiderate; and ourselves, when we overindulge or under-perform.

We mismanage our resources. We fish as a game—killing and wasting potential for food, oils, and so on. We hunt for a hobby—not using our kills. We bulldoze the forests for living areas while destroying our rainfalls. We manufacture beauty products, discharging waste chemicals that pollute our environment and weaken the ozone layer of our atmosphere.

As we continue to satisfy our wants and needs, we deliberately and carelessly violate natural and spiritual laws. We, at these times, act with seared consciences. For developers buy unsurveyed lands which they develop, cut, and sell as plots or lots for profit. With dynamite we blow up the sides of mountains for mining coal, gold, and diamond. We cut down large trees for wood and paper products. Then we waste the wood in the furniture factories and the paper in business offices and schools.

Some cities implemented policies which allow killing off hundreds of specific animals, birds, or bugs. The cities are then infested by another predator—the prey of the murdered species the policies allowed to be killed. The Chinese killed the sparrows that eat locusts. Then the locusts preyed on their corn crops—just as a thirsty man from the desert raids the first water hole he meets. In Charles Darwin's "The Origin Of Species," he has shown how one insect may eat from a plant, while either destroying or pollinating it. This insect may be eaten by a predator. The predator may then be eaten by a small animal and that animal by a larger and so the cycle continues from predator to prey.

Every plant or animal has a part to play in the drama of life. We cannot think of one as more important than the other, nor choose one that is more needful or has a greater purpose in the scheme of things. Our life experiences have shown that all have vital roles.

How we treat our environment is a measure of our effectiveness as caretakers of the earth. If we flatten the mountains to build cities and extend housing programs for profit, we have also exposed life in the valleys to the strong winds, hurricanes, and heat that the mountains and trees blocked out. If we drill for oil in the ocean for fuel and gas, we scare the fishes away.

Every act has a consequence. How we react to the consequence is another cause itself that will produce a following effect. The law of causality is never more demonstrated than when we interfere with any of the natural and environmental existences. Caution and forethought must come before our actions on our surroundings.

We own no land, sea, animal, plant, air-space—not even our bodies and souls. All are special gifts. All are loans while we live on earth. We must therefore treat our environment with an understanding of the economy of life. We must be ready to maintain balance while we act causing as little as possible destruction.

This destruction, however, is not always evil or sinful. Builders break down a house to rebuild; gardeners disturb the weeds and earthworms when ploughing their lands to sow their crop seeds; the surgeons cut human flesh to remove cysts; the businessmen may lay off workers to avoid bankruptcy; we sacrifice now to use energy and resources later.

Sacrifice is a type of destruction, for it hinders in its duration specific wants and needs from fulfilment. Such a fulfilment is an expectation, a hope that sacrifice destroyed. As with this instance, destruction is often a misnomer. While arson and booming are wrong and illegal, demolition of a building is needed if we must rebuild a better, more secure, and more spacious, living facility. This principle can be illustrated with many so-called destructive act. It has been well stated by a sage as "whatever may do good may do harm" and "the same sun that hardens the clay softens the wax."

Note that the action of the object or the sun above is neither good nor evil. Note also that the object or the sun is neither an evil nor a good thing. The Old Testament well illustrates this universal principle. God told Jehu to "...destroy the house of Ahab" (2 Kings 9;:7). But Jehu became overzealous and went beyond his limits (2 Kings 10:11), for he killed Ahab's servants, best friends, and priests as well. Though the command to take life was from God, Jehu's excessive killing was disobedience. But we learn that Jehu will pay for his excessive, forbidden, and evil action (Hosea 1:4). We also see that while taking a life was against one of God's commandments, God ordered blood to be shed. We may argue that He is God. He created all. Therefore, all life belongs to Him and He can do as He pleases. That to me, though true, is not the act of a benevolent, perfect, God.

I would much prefer an impersonal God who is fair, loving and merciful. Who created all laws and is omnipresent. If Ahab's family violated several divine decrees, then by the teaching, loving, and divine laws such persons must account and learn to discontinue their sinful and evil ways. When they paid their dues by the hands of Jehu, it was a natural and divine response for them to make adjustment by the fate dealt to them for their wrongs. But Jehu went beyond his inner directives, and in so doing, he has violated an inner, divine prompting. Now, he too, has put a burden on his conscience from which he must be redeemed.

However, whether Jehu's story was true or allegorical, it will not reduce the principle—though severely illustrated—that the killing was first used to carry out a divine law of compensation; but in Jehu's over-anxiousness, excessive killing was evil.

This point is well made by our court and justice system today. The law enforcement officer is empowered to use firearms during his course of duties. He is also allowed to use "reasonable force" as he arrests an alleged criminal. If he uses too much force; if he kills or uses his firearms "unreasonably or excessively," he becomes guilty of a criminal act. Thus, the Attorney General authorizes law enforcers to use guns, when necessary, in carrying out their duties. But killing is against the law of the land.

Causality is also well illustrated with the shortages we see in our world today. We have wasted so much, that now we must accept the consequence of our actions. Natural, spring water is on sale in stores. Years ago, we went to any stream and freely take as much as we wanted as well as needed. Now fresh spring water is becoming scarce.

We have been paying for water many years now as a major utility in our homes supplied by the Hydro companies. They use this water to give us heat and electricity. Will we have to pay for the supply of oxygen in the future? What a ridiculous thought, you say! But we may have reacted similarly years ago, if someone mentioned that we may be buying water in our groceries and convenience stores. Even so, in emergency cases, oxygen is supplied in sealed containers which the hospitals must buy. The thought is not so ridiculous any more.

The compensation we are receiving for violating nature's laws seems more severe as time goes by. Although shortages are teaching us how to better coexist with nature, our stubbornness is causing us to learn only by increasingly harsher lessons.

Is Conscience God

"Let conscience be your guide," has been an admonition for years. Many persons prefer it to "Let Jesus be your guide," or "Let God be your guide." The reason for this preference may be due to our human herd instinct that makes popularity proof of truth. For when we are overwhelmed by the general acceptance of a view, its popularity and repetition give it an apparent weight in soundness.

But we have said that the generality of an opinion does not prove the opinion to be true. We must strive always to flood ourselves with the superstate of Christ Consciousness, with God's Holy Spirit. In this way, we feed directly from God's universal love and wisdom. We can, therefore, direct our lives in harmony with His decrees and His laws; for God's directives are reliable. Thus our appraisals will be in harmony with universal truths.

Christians are not confused about who to follow. We are not confused about whose directives is right and whose is wrong. We are always sure when we follow the dictates of God. And when we are in doubt about any matter, we only have to read God's word, the Christian Holy Bible, and we know the right yardstick to use—the right values to uphold.

In society, the word conscience—among many others—has often replaced the word God. Many who declare their disbelief in God, their disbelief in His power and might, use the word conscience where the theist will use the word God. Conscience, to these unbelievers, these atheists, is their ultimate guide to right and wrong. Thus, "Let conscience be your guide," for them, is the best and highest moral value of which man is capable.

These persons must admit that such a view suggests that conscience is an authority on moral issues. Their persistence to maintain this perception implies that, to them, the judgments of conscience are infallible, for their view affirms that conscience must have the last say.

This obvious regard for conscience as the highest authority displays such persons's acknowledgement that man must yield to a set of supreme characteristics or a set of traits that transcend human, ordinary capabilities.

Added to this observation, on two occasions I was asked by different individuals, why is God necessary? Both were friends. They wanted to know why do we need God or the idea of God? I never had an answer to really satisfy them. I do not know if I really can find one. To simply hand them a Christian Bible and say, "This is God's word. Read it and you will find the answers to your question," is not enough.

I can tell them to pray and ask God for guidance, so that He may reveal Himself or an answer to them. For God said, "You will seek me and find me when you seek me with all your heart. [And I] will bring you back from captivity…from…places where I have banished you to the place from which I carried you into exile" (Jeremiah 29:13-14). But this too will not suffice. And what is more, I am assuming they accept that God exists, for this assumption is the central premise of their question.

Even if I presumptuously leave the whole issue on the inner premise that I will pray for them and God in due time will reveal it to them, this too is not acceptable. I will be presuming, in the first place, that in some way that I have a grasp of "things" that are too deep for their current understanding. Secondly, I will be presuming that they have not matured spiritually enough to acquire that personal relation with God. Thirdly, I will be presuming that my prayer will undoubtedly be answered. Finally, I again presume—probably in error—that they accept that God exists. What presumptions!

It is clear that with the advance of technology, especially in the medical sciences, humans find it difficult to acknowledge God's existence. The assumptions and fears of early humans have been despelled by the new light and knowledge acquired through self and environmental explorations.

Yesterdays impossibilities are done today—and with much ease. Many of the physiological conditions and diseases we did not understand and could not cure, we can do so now. We no longer need spiritual healings in some areas as medical science have found the cures for such illnesses.

The development of computer and data technology are also helping us to rapidly understand our surroundings and ourselves. For this technology has accelerated our findings in research and development. It may be that the rapidity of change confuses us in such a manner that we forget the prime force causing it. Our understanding is blocked because we are too occupied with adapting to the rapid changes and thus we forget the little but important things. Our mental state is like that of a worried man so absorbed in his cares that he forgets his manner when a passer by say "hello" to him.

The volume of new knowledge from our discoveries is so much to absorb that we find it takes much of our time. We forget to sit and be thankful for what we are learning and for the benefits we are receiving.

Let us not say that those who deny God's existence are ungrateful. But let us say without a doubt that they show ingratitude to someone or something for the new knowledge they received. Even here we again presume God's existence and our statement does not still answer the question of God's necessity. After all, the Christian Bible admonishes that "we prove all things" first before we accept them as true (1 Thessalonians 5:21). Thus questioning the very existence and if so, the necessity of God is healthy.

The car, the aeroplane, the telephone, and other electronic and mechanical devices have been invented and we do not have the inventors around today nor remember them. Yet we are using their creations and benefits. We do not need them now, but were it not for their work, we would not have had the level of progress we have today. We are certainly in their debt and are greatful for their efforts.

As a result, we honour them today with statues, places in our museums, and by recording their achievements in our archives. Some of us study them and are motivated by their efforts and trials. In this sense, they are ever alive. We are similarly affected by the train and aeroplane drivers we do not see. The service they provide we need even though we may never personally meet them or thanked them.

These examples illustrate a kind of perceptual relationship that many theists have with their idea of God. They assume and believe He created the world and all there is and so they revere and honour Him. They believe due to their personal experience that He provides for all their current needs—especially as science cannot explain many occurrences. As humans are teleological by nature, we believe that someone or something must be the cause for all happenings— particularly the inexplainable. However, the theist cannot prove God's existence any more than the atheist can disprove it. To the former, God is real.

There are obviously some realities we cannot prove to another by accepted scientific means. Take the coincidences of two persons having the same tune in their minds simultaneously. The experience is real to each yet neither can prove it to the other. To me and to others God exists. Perhaps our agreement in belief is but a mere coincidence.

Underlying the above contentions is the universal fact that mind thinks, conceives, and synthesizes. Thus no matter who denies the above assumptions and in what manner, mind exist to cause knowledge and awareness. In fact, it is mind that allows us to deny and to accept. To take this argument elsewhere, I confess I do not know what could have created the first mind force. I leave this to those who grapple with ontological questions and I will only express my wonder.

In Particle Physics, there is the theory that all is vibratory. But this is not new to students of mysticism and philosophy who, did not have any "mundane scientific way" to prove their views. Now if we consider our universe as being a mass of vibrations, we must wonder the possibility of these interacting to result in a specific arrangement call mind. We must also wonder about the origin of these initial vibrations and what must have propelled them as well.

We are getting no closer to the ultimate cause of all with our line of thinking or to the proof of the existence of spiritual essence. I can only assume the existence of a primary mind force. I say force as all life comprise of activity of different kinds. And force is integral to activity, we cannot have one without the other.

The Big Bang and other theories must account for the existences prior to the bang, and how these existences came into being, as well as what force propelled them. Certainly these occurrences could not have just appeared from "nothing" or "no thing." Even the Chaos theories must account similarly. But I am unqualified to argue along the line of particle physics theories and the like.

For now, we do know that we are here on earth. We know that we are "alive"—the word we use to describe the state of how we exist. The Bible assumes the same conditions, for in Genesis, we are never told how God came into being. We are only told that God exists and He created us into existence. Now many people personify God. This may be due to the statement that we are created in his image. But one can just as well refer to Him as a Mind Force. A car by any other name is still a car. Our acknowledging it or denying it will not change it or its nature or make it non-existent.

When we look at human being through the eyes of experience and scientific knowledge, we find that there are mental activities, thoughts, and incidents for which we cannot explain by physical laws and common experiences. It is also highly presumptuous to say we will never be able to provide any satisfactory explanation. We only have to remember the first aeroplane, the telephone, and other inventions in history and we see how man is still making possible today what was impossible yesterday.

Perhaps the possibility of developing a device to receive and interpret "psychic or spiritual impressions" is in the making. Who knows? It probably already exists. Let us not laugh this away and later be laughed at like history's many *doubting Thomas's*.

There are many of us who dream about tomorrows and "see" future incidents. To group these experiences as "freak occurrences" and "mere accidents" is to blatantly disregard the lessons of the past. Simply because we have no known objective method to prove them do not warrant our saying they are foolish and are tricks of the imagination.

But the world has had its laughs time and again on those so-called doubting, scientific authorities who criticized each new major development and condemned them as improbable or impossible. Many accidents can be traced to somebody's choice and decision accompanied by carelessness or ignorance. We are no longer scared of thunders as audible displays of God's anger. We know their causes and their effects.

We must continue to search for rational answers to claims of "predictive dreams" or "psychic occurrences." For since they embody ideas, images, and emotions of what is going to happen, then there is evidence that mind and consciousness are involved.

If we argue that it is the tricks of our own minds which somehow form these future conclusions, then we admit that these psychic or spiritual occurrences have some kind of reality. Further, when some of these predictions and psychic occurrences turn out to be true, we can no longer cast them aside as lucky conjectures, or cheap deceptions.

The type of mental activity involved in psychic experiences, we need to investigate. Psychology has already named such mental activities subconscious. But because we do not know how to wilfully access or harness their "finer" impressions does not mean that they are unreliable. After all, there were much trials and errors before any device was reasonably perfected.

We often display our human vanity when we presume in words or attitudes, that if we are unaware of a law, principle, or incident, then it must either be unreal or a mental delusion. Our inability to access the services of our subconscious at will does not mean that subconscious activities are unreal, fallible, or unreliable. We behave today no differently than when we had just begun to discover light, radio waves, and how to build safe aeroplanes.

Subconscious activity is truly a realm that we need to explore just as we venture deep into the cosmos, the seas, and the human, physical body. It is within this realm we place our virtues, values, highest morals, and judgments. This realm is the invisible thought world in which we harbour our deepest fears, highest aspirations, and righteous or valuable conceptions. Herein lies our truest self—the self that is the best we can be.

Though this self changes with experience and education; though it is constructive and positive; though it strives always for peace and harmony; we know that we do not create all its notions. Many of our inner promptings and impellings must have come from a higher self, because of their benevolence and high standards. Since many of us have these same illumination, then this higher self has a universal character. For often it is common for more than two persons to have the same enlightenment although they may be miles apart.

This experience is similar to the everyday occurrence of two televisions receiving from one main station. We may call the higher self absolute reality, absolute mind, or God. Since God is to each of us a personal realization, conception, or perception, we may say, like some mystical students and the Christian writer Andrew Murray, God of our hearts.

Perhaps, it is only our stubbornness and at times the confusing our bad experiences with religious dogma why we ask, Is God necessary? This question, though, has a positive side. It helps us to really reaffirm a cosmic and spiritual reality.

For we can look at the plants, the seas, the animals, the cosmos, and ourselves and begin questioning and arrive at reasonable answers why a God is necessary. And for me, because God exists as cosmic energy and mind force it is the reason we can know anything. The more we improve the more we depend and use this Cosmic mind and energy.

The development of society and man is proof of our greater harmony with this ultimate source of knowledge. Many inventions came intuitively. Many discoveries, means that which was discovered was there, already in existence. What motivated or prompted man to go left or right to discover? What in our mental syntheses presented the "long time missing link" that creates for us the new condition, invention, or product?

Even our notions of right and wrong has changed over time. Generally speaking, we no longer pray to idols; we no longer behead another human whose religious values differ from our own; we are still learning to be tolerant and to respect the views of others—no matter how contradictory they may seem to us. We have not perfected these levels of tolerance and open-mindedness yet; but our present efforts are sure demonstrations of our capacity to love one another, and to respect differences.

If we did not have these ideas of goodness before, from where did they arise? Where do we or our conscience get these godlike virtues? Could it be mere coincidence if each of our individual consciences have similar virtues? We often use coincidences as either an excuse when we are stubborn to acknowledge a principle, law, or an application of one of these that is unknown to us.

Without some common standards, we would have no society. Coincidence or not, many of us do have similar perceptions of virtues. It is these commonalities that also give rise to the notions of the existence of a universal, single, and ubiquitous consciousness resident in all men and women alike.

As Christians we will undoubtedly have similar virtues as we all drink from the same fountain of knowledge—Christ Consciousness or Christ Spirit (Colossians 3:3,4). The question is if the similar virtues we find in Christianity and other religions, is because those religions also drink from the same fountain of knowledge as we do.

Perhaps this fountain is called by different names. After all, if "A" is a set of qualities we get when we associate with "B." And "C" has the same qualities call "A." It is reasonable to assume that "C" somehow was associated with "B." Because of some variations we can say that "A" and "C" may be different expressions of "B." But both expressions or truth claims cannot be true.

Christians know that Christ wants us to become a branch of His vine which is planted and taken care of by God. For Christ wants us to receive all that he receives. Thus all our thoughts and actions will be in accord with God as He and God are one (John 10:30). In our unity with Christ, we can show true brotherhood and sisterhood.

Therefore, we can respect each other. When we try to rid our society of racial discrimination, prejudices, dogmatism, and other similar mental diseases, we will be determining values and standards from one common, perfect source.

Conscience, though used as a synonym to God or used in place of God by some, is not opposed to God. Because it is so popularly acknowledged, conscience implies a universal reality. We note too that it encourages good behaviour, consistency, and self harmony. In an earlier chapter, we showed how conscience grows and becomes more humane, evolved, and respectful. We said that conscience strives through its evolution towards perfection.

Let us remember that any notion of perfection describes the characteristics of the God Idea. Though the Idea of God may be subjected to change, this does not necessarily mean that God is imperfect. Energy, for instance, changes but still remains indestructible. Science tells us that energy may be one form today and another tomorrow, but in each form it is still vibratory. This indestructibility of energy, regardless of its forms, is likened to the perfection and permanence of God—no matter its conception or perception.

To disbelieve in God's existence, and to believe in a conscience is inconsistent in reason, logic, and experience. For if conscience is the Highest Judge of a person, as some say, and it is always right, then conscience has been given perfect, absolute, and immortal values.

Are these not the values the theists say are of God? Further, if such values reside in the conscience of all men alike, are we not saying that there lies in all men an intelligence and consciousness that is perfect and is in harmony? Thus we have given this so-called "conscience" the qualities of God.

Here lies the confusion. What then is the matrix that suggests to us today and we feel good; but on the same issue tomorrow suggests differently and we sure the latter suggestion is right? Sure this suggester is not perfect. Therefore it cannot be God. Conscience, we saw from previous chapters changes; it evolves. It at times may prompt us to a course of action that differs from what it had encouraged in the past—because it has grown, it has become more humane, and benevolent.

Our experience in life shows us that there are persons of weak, strong, seared and clear conscience or at least they demonstrate instances of each of these types of conscience. The inexperienced is easily swayed to any action; the knowledgeable is determined and sticks to his or her "guns"; the criminal sleeps well after a crime; the virtuous is usually without guilt for he or she forever makes peace with himself or herself.

This relative good displayed by our conscience is proof of how undependable our conscience can be as a judge of ultimate values. We have seen earlier that we must train conscience if we want it to function effectively. Thus if we fill it with specific kinds of values, it would use such values as parts of its measuring rod.

Conscience reminds us of the computer expression garbage in garbage out. If our conscience is God, then we would not need to train it. Further, if we feel it contains the highest good of which we are capable, to train it and change its standards suggest that our perception of the highest good has changed. We do not need to train that which is perfect. Instead, it is that which is perfect that can train us.

Experience proves we all have different standards and thus different expressions of conscience. If there is a universal mind and consciousness of God resident in all of us call soul, then our conscience only reflects the degree of clarity we perceive of this spiritual essence.

The Bible says that "…the blood of Christ through the eternal spirit" will "…cleanse our conscience from acts that lead to death, so that we may serve the living God" (Hebrew 9:14). Some of the acts our conscience approves are not in harmony with God's decrees; therefore, our conscience needs cleansing by the blood of Christ through the Holy Spirit, if we must truly serve and benefit from God.

Clearly, conscience and God is neither in opposition, nor are they the same. According to the Bible, if conscience needs cleansing by God's Holy Spirit, we see here that conscience is not perfect and therefore cannot be God.

However, we need both God and conscience. God has created, in His love for us and in His knowledge of our imperfection, conscience. He has put in us this matrix of sensitivity and responsivity that has an accessible, permanent memory. It is associated with mind, consciousness, and incarnated soul personality. We cannot see nor touch it with our hands.

Thank God it is not an organ like the kidney or the heart that we can physically operate on. It is easy to imagine the implications if conscience were subject to the scalpel. We already have a degree of freedom when we put into it what we choose. Any more privileges would lead us to greater self-destruction.

Conscience has no size nor shape. We cannot say here it is or there it is. We cannot remove it if we wanted, nor can we change the principles of how or when it must function. It works automatically and continuously; and it neither sleeps nor tires. Once we are alive, conscience works. As we think, speak, or act, it clicks in, and does so again, when we have completed our expressions and when we review them later.

Conscience is subjected to our will to the extent that it is a container within which we can place our morals, ethics, values, and standards. Therefore, we can choose what we put in or take out. It is our data bank with a reliable memory—not righteous judgement. It is sensitive and responsive while it uses the information we put in it.

When we repent, it is because our conscience has been tormenting us. Repentance is an emotional and spiritual experience. It occurs when we realize that we have violated our standards and universal laws. We are also aware of the consequences of our actions. Thus we realize our sinful and evil ways with their complementary painful repercussions.

We feel the intensity of the pains we caused and we immediately know in our consciousness the ethical and universal principles we breached. We submit and cooperate with God's decree during this occurrence. We had done wrong and we know and feel it.

Our conscience reacts only upon the strengths of its contents. Its reaction is perfect only if the contents we put in is perfect. If we place God's decrees in our conscience and we regularly review these by repetition until they become habits—the law and order of our lives—we will have no fear when we act or speak. Let conscience be your guide, is an incomplete admonition. It needs the conditional clause, "when its contents are in harmony with God's precepts." Thus we should say, "Let conscience be your guide, when its contents are in harmony with God's precepts."

Adventure with Conscience

I have always had much trouble with the meaning of Christmas. I felt it was only natural for me to dream about it.

Conscience disallows me to accept Santa Claus as the central figure of Christmas, though the principle of giving is made alive with him. The great commercializing of Christmas turns me off, though much gifts to one another is a good fervour, and should be practised all year round. Yet we must be grateful for even this small measure: that the world is united in the spirit of brotherhood and to some greater degree, the memory of the Christ.

I laboured, reasoned, and searched my mind, until the law was fulfilled: I imagined an angel appeared to me saying, "You have been given an appointment by your Lord, God Almighty. You must tell others about your Christmas dream. We have watched you sincerely hunting its true meaning. You have for yourself found much truth; but it is time for additional principles to be given to you."

I was scared, hesitant, and confused. I could not honestly say if this is a dream, a vision, or a trick of the mind. I simply casted the imagery away; but for the rest of the week, this experience stayed in my mind. As I sat on my couch one evening after work, and tried to read my Bible, I dozed of—which so often happens. In between the borderline state of sleep and wake, I heard myself saying, "Yes! I must dream of Christmas."

At once I felt a peace come over me, and that I am in all things.

Then a presence—a comforting, peaceful presence enshrouded me. My soul became calm and serene; my burdens and concerns were no more. My Lord and my Christ was with me. I knew it but could not explain how. "O Perfect Love, how sweet thou are." O how my imperfect soul rejoiced; my heart fluttered. I could not behold his total presence: as did Peter, James, and John—only a glimpse. I wanted so much to have more, to realize more; but as a young branch, my capacity was limited. I must slowly grow with time, as the life sap from his vine feeds me and I become a large enough branch to imitate his vine and share and bear fruits: for this is my only purpose.

Now a voice: whispering, sweet, soft, and gentle voice, yet authoritative, began to speak: "I am Christmas. I do not have a white beard and a snow-white hair. I do not wear a bright red hat with a lily white pompon, nor do I have a red coat and a Scottish red skirt edged with white cotton. Nor do I wear a black belt with a large and sparkling silver buckle. And black shoes, I have none.

Moreover, my place of abode is neither cold nor hot. Do not look for me in the skies riding a golden chariot with reindeers pulling me. With elves and bears in front and after me, helping me. Oh no! You will not find me with such company or in such activities. Nor will you find me climbing down the chimney, invading a family's privacy. Do not waste sleepless nights with such expectations.

When you need me, I shall be there for you. Time and space I know not. Past, present and future I know not. All is one and the same to me. There is no change for I am here and I am there at once. I am the true Christmas. I do not come once per year; but all year round: every month, week, day, hour, minute, second, moment. I am divine. I am the Son of God, your saviour, your only intercessor to God. I am your life. I am your only hope to enter my Father's Heavenly kingdom; and you will be a citizen there only if I approve you, if I convict you.

Your house, your car, your millions of dollars—do not call these your greatest gifts. Your life, your body, your soul, your power to choose, and even your divine spirit are also not your greatest gifts. Only God can give you the greatest gift. And He has given it everlastingly. Did He not give you me, His only begotten Son; because He loves you?

But I love you too. I taught you, died for you, cried for you, sacrificed for you. My body I gave you as bread to eat. You ate it and suffered in my name and you are blessed. It is the substance of your spiritual temple—a composite of your spiritual clothing. It is holy.

My blood is your living water. It cleanses, it reconciles, it sanctifies, it unites you with the Father, it gives you eternal life. I bought you with my blood. With it, I conquered death, I conquered satan; and so have you.

My soul is righteous. It is the righteousness you seek. My Father will give you all things, if you seek my soul. Let it be your well and fountain. Such blessings as you abide in me, will be given unto you as you ask in my name and act with my Christ—like will and soul. Such abiding will make my character your character and yours mine; my attitudes yours and yours mine; my joys yours and yours mine. You and I shall be one. Hallelujah, Hallelujah, Hallelujah. Hosanna in the highest. Glory to God.

"My spirit you can have free for I am your Christmas gift. I said I shall pour it out to you and I do not lie. I live for my Father and He cannot lie so I cannot lie. Whatever I say I mean and will do, for my words are my Father's as I abide in Him. As you hide in me, in him, my spirit makes your words law; so you too will not lie. So bathe and let my spirit move you. Oh let it incite you, let it take charge of you. Be a child unto it.

I am Christmas, your true Christmas. And remember when you abide in me, my Father, your Father is pleased. Seek not my pleasures; but the Father's. I and He are one. Work for him, not for me; for I too work for him. Pray to him, not to me; for I too pray to him. Do as I do because I know my Father better than you; but he is your Father too.

At Christmas, your act of giving is an act of love. I am that love, for the Father and I are one and He is love. When you give to another, do not feel proud and await thanks; for the heart does not receive thanks for pumping its body's blood; the hands do not feel joy in washing its body; nor do the feet in taking the body from place to place; nor the eyes, for showing what is ahead; nor the ears, for hearing the surroundings.

They all are part of the same body. They all are working in harmony for growth and longevity. How can you expect rewards when each is dependent on one another and none is greater than the other. If you are part of the same body—my body, for I am the Christ,—how can you thank yourselves for helping a part of yourself? Am I not your heart wherein lies gratitude, and your mouth from which thankfulness is uttered?

From dust all came and to dust all will return. You came with nothing and will return with nothing. You created nothing. How can you give to another what does not belong to you? All you have is borrowed. If you and another are one, then what you have the other has. And how can you give to him that which is already his?

It is sensible to give to oneself. But that is not giving, but helping oneself. Still, it is not helping but doing for oneself: hence it is one's duty and thus a law. To give to another who is also a part of the body of Christ is duty and law.

My Father has given me and I have given you. I have been given authority and domain over all. And all that I have, I offer to you freely, only if you do as I do. Glorify the Father. Praise God. Listen to me, for I know Him best, so if you follow me, I assure you my Father will be pleased. I cannot lie; for I am one with my Father and lying is an abomination to Him. He hates it.

I am not a myth, nor am I a fantasy. I am. I am real. I am actual.

I am the true Christmas. When you celebrate me and say, "Merry Christmas"; celebrate not my soul personality, but my acts of obedience to God; celebrate not what I have done, but what I have been privileged to have the Father do through me. I am now Lord of all by the love and authority of the Father. You can do miracles in my name and glorify the Father, for He is showing what power, what possibilities when He showers His love unto those who obey Him. I obey Him. Oh! I am the true Christmas, the only true Christmas."

This then is the end of my dream. If I trained my conscience with

God's word, though I make my great share of errors and sins; the more I put His words in my heart, my heart and conscience will reject only that which is against God's principles. Once I re-read what I have written and found many scriptures consistent with it; then I can be sure that "the Master Within or Inner Guardian," would find harmony with my story and so not object to it.

If I now further seek my Lord and in my "stillness" I listen to His whisperings and I obey Him, then I know that not my conscience; but His Grace was upon my works for I have indeed glorified Him with my efforts.

I cannot prove to another that I know; but my brothers and sisters in Christ with me and those who understand the meaning of the "idea-force called the Body of Christ," will know that I had a confirmation. For all who walk with the Lord and thread the path know the technical applications needed for success and the salvation of the soul.

Yes, my spirit rejoices in the indwelling of the Holy Spirit in me; it rejoices for this adventure with conscience; it realizes more of its actual and dormant truths. I now have peace profound.

Confusion with Conscience

Most of us have mistaken the actions of our character from the work of our conscience. We view and refer to them interchangeably. They both are so alike in expressions when we live through them, that it is often difficult to discern one from the other. The result is confusion; the reason, ignorance. We have been doing this so long in society and in our private lives that most persons take the use and meaning of the word conscience for granted. Many public speakers and politicians, who are obviously sceptic, cynic, agnostic, or atheist; and even many Bible believing pastors would often make the same statement of claim: "I know that my conscience is clear." From our previous chapters, we know now that the point of reference—the set of morals upon which each of their consciences are based—may differ greatly.

We tend to use the word conscience out of context. For instance, the values and morals of persons of different religious systems vary. Since the operations of our conscience are rooted in our morals, clearly the standards that make up a strong conscience for a Christian will differ somewhat from those that will be the basis of a strong conscience for a Hindu, a Buddhist, or someone from another religious system. Further, even a strong conscience for an evangelical Christian would have some variation from those of a Mormon or even a Roman Catholic. In this book, I reiterate that conscience has been written and defined from an evangelical Christian context.

Words often cause problems in communication and understanding. This is mainly so when we use them inappropriately. Besides contextual problems, we are challenged to use words denotatively or connotatively correct. We confuse conscience and determination or strong will, when we observe a persistent person whose mind is set on a specific goal or endeavour. We confuse conscience with charity and brotherly kindness, when we say the person is "*soft-hearted.*" We confuse conscience with even altruism, when we comment on how others consciously and sacrificially respond to the needs of their fellows. "Their hearts have gone out to the people," we might say. Or we may conclude, "they have a *heart of gold.*"

Strong Willed (determined) or Strong Conscience

Is having a strong conscience the same as being strong willed? First of all, the person with a strong conscience is one we have said whose mind, *hearing*, and *eyesight* is set on God. Such persons are truly Christ-like and will always imitate the character of Christ. These individuals are humble and submissive always to God's laws and ordinances. It is indeed a mystery and a conundrum, in Christianity, to define strength and the power of God with a imagery of a helpless Christ on the cross. But it is at the foot of the cross where the heart of the person with a strong conscience is "*placed.*" They are neither weaklings nor fools. They can think for themselves, learn from their experiences, and formulate their own personal views too. When it comes to a clear matter of obedience to God's rulings, they are "pig-headed." God's Word is the truth and it is unquestionable and infallible. They know only one reaction, one behaviour, one commitment: do as the Almighty commands—whether it is painful to do so or not.

These persons do not change their minds or their positions for they know what they are doing and they know that their positions are backed by the will of God. Their positions are based on God's Word. Herein lie their stubbornness and their apparent self-opinionatedness. But being self-opinionated on issues wherein one takes the side of God is to be on the winning side—and that side is the true majority. A person with a strong conscience is humble but with a indomitable spirit. They yield, but only to the power and might of God as well as to His love. They are sympathetic; but not to the point of changing their positions to disobedience with God's laws to please others. They read and meditate on the scriptures daily.

Let us look at the strong willed. Such characters show fortitude and are irresolute in their positions. Persons with strong wills would not change their minds or views—no matter the consequences. They are belligerent. They are not ones with whom we would normally choose to argue. They do not compromise or seem cooperative at all. They are also stubborn. If they have sympathy for our views and emotions, they do not seem to allow that sympathy to move them to the point where they will change their vote. They are "as stubborn as a mule" the saying goes. They are inflexible.

Now persons who are determined to do something, means that they have already decided. Mentally, therefore, their determination is their fuel, their propulsion system. They have already analysed and reasoned. Note that when they decide on a matter, they will not waiver or give up, but see it through. Determination is their resolve. The determined persons have checked with their standards and had "the permission" or "the go-ahead." Determination has nothing to do with right or wrong; rather, it is the will power to persist. Their entire being and posture support their positions or convictions. Determination is like a tool or perhaps mule—it can be used for good or ill.

The process of checking our standards to arrive at a conclusion describes the initial work of our conscience. Next, as previously stated, our conscience confers a value to its conclusion and expresses this value as regret, guilt, remorse, or approval. The decision to apply this conclusion and the persistence—no matter the obstacles—to see it through is determination. Clearly, determination cannot be the same as our conscience. For determination is firmness, resoluteness. It is the attitude, the mentality, and the enactment of a viewpoint. On the other hand, conscience evaluates and expresses its judgement. Determination is in our actions; whilst conscience is involved in our reactions to the impulses it receives.

For analogy, let us think of the operation of nuclear missiles. We have read that once the missile is programmed for a target, and it is fired, it locks-on the target. It maintains its collision course despite the target's manoeuvring. Determination is like a programmed behaviour. A person might be determined to carry out a specific action plan. Regardless of the consequences or obstacles, the determined person pursues the objective to completion. It can also be illustrated when the predator picks up the scent of his prey. It tracks its prey over long distances—persistently in pursuit of captivity or for the kill. The locking-on to a target, the persistence of the hunt for the prey is determination.

Christianity is a religious system of love, compassion, and peace. Christ, even at the point of death and excruciating pain, prayed for God to forgive his persecutors. He was innocent. Judas Iscariot said he had caused innocent blood to be shed, as he betrayed his master—Jesus the Christ. To be Christ-like is to operate from a strong conscience. Yes, such a person is indeed strong willed and determined, but ONLY in their submission and obedience to God's Will. They are unselfish and put the good of others before their own, in accord to the Holy Scriptures. Their consciences are strong as it is ever in unison and in sync with God.

Just as the missile can be obstructed before it impacts its target, and the predator can lose its scent during the hunt for its prey, so can determination wane or weaken at times.

But persons of strong consciences will not waiver and they will carry their crosses to the end—despite the trials and tribulations—and receive the reward of the crown of righteousness or glory, according to the apostles Paul and Peter (2 Tim. 4:8; 1 Pet. 5:4). The strong willed person is a determined person. This individual is driven by belief or knowledge with related emotions or passion. Such a person may either have a seared or strong conscience. Whichever it is, they push forward.

That being said, we must not confuse strong willed and strong conscience. The person with strong conscience, we have said, has the characteristic of the strong will or is determined. Unlike the mere determined personality, the person of strong conscience will not surrender to any difficulties except to the Law of Jesus Christ. They are loyal to the point of death. Observe the list of Christian martyrs over the centuries. Further, we can be strong willed about the right or wrong thing. So being strong willed is one of the qualities of our character. It is not a faculty in itself that decides, chooses, analyses, or evaluates. A strong will *is not* a consciousness or intelligence as *is* our conscience.

Kindness and Strong Conscience

What about kindness: is this the same as strong conscience? We may say someone has a good or strong conscience when they are kind. But when two criminals are on a crime scene, do they not help each other? After all, teamwork here too gets the job done more efficiently. I am not concerned with the type of activity, but to simply illustrate the point of 'brotherly kindness.' It is not my intention here to profane a creaturely good.

To be kind, is to be helpful. It is to meet the needs of another, following sympathy for the other person's state. The person helped may or may not ask; but once we offer and give aid voluntarily, this is kindness. A soldier may dislike one of his peers; but when the common enemy approaches, he fights in unison and would help his wounded peer against the common threat.

The motivators or reasons in kindness are many. But we can group them into two major behavioural classes: one is ethical, the other, moral. The ethical is based on the spirit of accepted codes, rules, and regulations; while the moral, on the benefits and the good of humankind. Two professionals may facilitate each other—in compliance with their professional code of ethics. This has nothing to do with their love for each other as brothers and sisters. The former behaviour is governed by a man made organizational code and standard. The latter is empowered by our unity in Christ, as part of a body bonded by selfless love.

Kindness is not conscience, but one of the many of the personal characteristics of our soul personalities. If we put into our hearts the law and habit of doing for another voluntarily and without expectation of any returns, when an opportunity arises we will simply have the urge to show kindness. Paul encourages us to be kind to one another.

Does this confusion exist because kindness is a virtue and a strong conscience is Christ-like thus fostering a kind nature itself? We often say, "the kind person has a *heart of gold.*" What a choice phrase; for gold is hard, yet pure. By this phrase, however, we allude to the purity and honesty of the individual's general conduct. Another phrase we use as a synonym to *heart of gold* is *pure heart.* Gold being a pure and valuable element, we naturally imply that such pure hearted persons, are honest, sincere, fair-minded, and particularly understanding.

Thus the pure hearted and kind person is obviously a description of the general character and virtuous behaviour of the person. Like strong will and determination above, kindness does not possess a consciousness and intelligence like that of conscience. It is just a classification or name given to a behaviour type. It is a value attributed to a behaviour of an individual. We look at what the person has done, and then we confer a value upon their deed—such as kindness.

Hardhearted or Seared Conscience

When Shylock in Shakespeare's "Merchant Of Venice" demanded his pound of flesh from Antonio, we say Shylock was *hardhearted* and thus without sympathy or compassion. What manner of a person as a lender, who will draft and enforce an agreement with a desperate borrower and in it, include a clause, demanding should the borrower fail to repay his debt on time, that the lender has a right to cut off one pound of flesh of the borrower? Can we put our minds back to the Bible and remember an outstanding display of hardheartedness in Exodus, of Remises, Pharaoh of Egypt? He did not want to free the Israelites from slavery no matter what the stated consequences of his disobedience to God. Was he strong willed? Yes, indeed—but about the wrong viewpoint—the enslavement of the Israelites—God's chosen people.

Again, hardheartedness is not the same as a seared conscience; though, it is a trait of a seared conscience. It is the value we ascribe to a display of a dispassionate characteristic. We call this *heartlessness* or we also say the person has *no heart*. Literally speaking, we know that according to human biology, someone cannot exist without a heart. Perhaps they can, if there is some kind of synthetic replacement to perform the same cardiovascular functions. I am unqualified to talk on this topic, but for the purpose of our discussions, it is sufficient to know that being without a heart, refers figuratively to the "*particular cold and insensitive trait*" of a person. One such demonstrable characteristic is the lack of compassion for others, God, or nature: **heartlessness** or **cold heartedness.**

We said that if an individual responds favourably or unfavourably to the suffering of another, we say the person is soft or hard hearted (or perhaps warm- or cold-hearted). Further, soft- or hardheartedness has strong overtones of being forgiving or unforgiving. These are two choice feelings describing our reactions when someone wrongfully hurts us and who was later penitent and wished to atone. The person whom we say is hard hearted, "without a heart," or "heartless," normally reacts cold and callus to human suffering. Such an individual will look directly at human affliction and will feel no need nor desire to help. This same person will not forgive another easily or at all.

Soft Hearted or Weak Conscience

The soft hearted person will not only empathize with human agony, but reach out with the intention to ease or remove the pains from his or her fellows. Such empathy is another characteristic of a strong conscience, while the disinterest in human suffering is a quality of a seared conscience.

There are occasions when we may describe someone as being fickle or weak. Here, we are referring to people who are easily influenced; that is, people who do not have any fixed "stand" on any issue. They waiver as leaves would in the varying direction of any wind. We say these people do not have a mind of their own or that they cannot or do not think for themselves.

Literally speaking, no one is mindless. No one lacks the free will to do one thing or another. Hence everyone can and do think—maybe not always critically. It is the doubt or ignorance in weak individuals that causes their indecision. These persons are easy victims of 'scripture twisters,' schemers, and false teachers. Sometimes, too, such persons may be too lazy or afraid to use reason and logic to form their own conclusion. Instead, they have developed the habit of relying on others to work things out for them. They replicate views without foundation; embrace beliefs without knowledge; and argue vociferously without reason or logic. This is undoubtedly a wrong practice and poor training for our mind.

The so-called weak person is without conviction and self confidence. They neither test nor prove rules or practices. They do whatever they are told or advised without checking the soundness of the instructions or counsels. They seem not to have established standards or values upon which their conscience must '*weigh*' its decision and response. Or at least the values they have are unsound and not supported by their own life experience. They may even question and doubt the verification they receive of a valid view. They often appear to be pliable which can be confused with compassion. But they are vulnerable and move in the direction of the stronger persuader or the most influential opinion.

But everyone has some type of value or standard. No conscience is void. These are given. Humans are forever receiving promptings from the universal consciousness of God, from their inner man, and the environment. And whatever we have read, heard, dreamt, or spiritually experienced are lodged in our memory. The knowledge and values from these are resident in our consciousness. From this consciousness, we also receive promptings.

With weak persons, they do not *trust* the values they have, they have not found justifications for them. Fear, superstitions, and delusions may cause them not to have any conviction about the lessons they learned from their own experiences.

If the weak person were to prove all things, test every spirit, put God's word into their hearts regularly, and develop healthy habits, then they will be building strong consciences. For fickleness is not the same as good conscience, but a characteristic of a weak conscience. A person with a weak conscience, we can say definitely, does not have strong will. For such a person can easily be persuaded to do the wrong thing, their views and opinions are not backed by universal truths or even valid objective reasoning. Their will is weak and so they waiver. They lack both revelation (it seems) and reason. Whatever they think or feel, is not branded in their souls. As if they have no scars with a quick reference memory that will bring to the fore of their conscious, objective minds, truths that they know by their intimate experiences.

Even when we say we have a peaceful mind or our conscience is not bothering us, we may be deluding ourselves. For a peaceful mind describes the harmony we currently feel. This does not mean that our conscience is truly clear. For if our actions are in accord with our values, we will feel this harmony—even if our values are morally wrong.

Thus if our conscience is seared and our actions harmonize with its values, we will feel no *immediate* torment. But as stated in earlier chapters, when we are quiet and unoccupied with the affairs of life, the voice of our Lord, the Holy Spirit, can now be heard—whispering through the silence and in the light of our evil actions. We may then feel the nudging and pangs of a tormented conscience. We explained earlier that it is at this point the hardhearted can become broken and ready to submit to God. This is the moment the hardhearted is brought to their knees at the foot of the Cross.

Peace of Mind or Clear Conscience

Prior to this, their minds were not restless. They were quite happy in their evil ways and were busy with laughter and the joy of the life they chose for themselves. Their actions cause no whipping from their consciences. Their conscience is as clear as the God fearing person with a strong conscience. To the first person with a hardened heart, they experience a delusion of a clear conscience; to the second, the calm they experience in their heart is real.

As discussed in the chapter, "The Nature Of Conscience," the clear conscience is a *relatively righteous* expression. We emphasize relative to suggest transient, unreal. Not only are the actions of this conscience in accord to the incumbent's perception of God's laws, but their expressions are truly *penitent*. So when we have a clear conscience, we acknowledge our imperfection; therefore we are always ready to apologise, repent, and atone. This expression of conscience is tricky. For our values may not necessarily be in accord to what is biblically sound, even though our feelings of penitence and desire to atone are sincere. This is indeed a trick of the mind, the heart, the devil. We are operating upon false premises.

When our minds and hearts are at ease and we experience no torment from our conscience, we conclude that our conscience is clear. We have peace of mind. We sleep well, and we have no nightmares. We are like pigs in a muddy sty. The animal is quite comfortable in the mess in which it lives. We, on the other hand, think it is filthy and we know it is indeed so. Unfortunately, the pigs never realise that it is—if they do, I am unaware if they can communicate this disapproval of how they live. But humans can. We can do like the Bereans and check to see if our perceptions are in line with the Scriptures. Thus when our conscience is clear, it has **Jesus' blood** stamp of approval.

What we often use as synonyms to conscience, are characteristics of either a strong, seared, weak, or clear conscience. We will normally refer to them as characteristics of our personality. It is important to differentiate the expressions of conscience from their characteristics or our personality traits if we intend to direct our lives to attain true material and spiritual benefits. Our conscience or heart, is not God; but a free gift of God. It is one of the creaturely good. Its purpose is to help to return us back to the sacred romance with God for which we were freely and lovingly created by Him in the first place. We need only to let conscience be grounded on Scripture and be influenced by the Holy Spirit.